MANAG YOUR MONEY, MASTER YOUR LIFE

10 PRACTICAL FINANCIAL CONCEPTS FOR ACHIEVING FINANCIAL INDEPENDENCE

SEZAIR JULIEN

Manage your money, master your life
© Copyright <<2021>> **Sezair Julien**

For more information, email sezjul@gmail.com.

ISBN: 978-1-7361719-0-5

Acknowledgement

I would like to dedicate this book to my lord and savior, Jesus Christ. You have created me with the purpose to teach and help others achieve their potential. Thank you for giving me the ability to apply these lessons and concepts in my life.

I would also like to dedicate this book to my wife, Clairina and my three kids, Serina, Stephen, and Daniel. I would like to thank you for your constant support, dedication, and understanding during this whole process of writing this book.

This book is also dedicated to my mother, Jesula, and my father, Charles Julien. You are my role models. Mom, even though you are not here, you will be in my heart forever You are the foundation of my financial education and my life.

Special thanks to all my mentors, teachers, brothers and sisters, sisters-in-law, brothers-in-law, nieces, and nephews.

Sezair Julien

Table of Contents

Part Four: Buying power (What can you afford?)

Introduction

Why I Wrote this book

Do you want to take charge of your finance? Are you tired of reading about financial freedom and not able to apply the knowledge? Then this book is for you. If you want to master your life, it is a requirement that you manage your money well. This book is written with you in mind. After losing my job in the 2008 financial crisis, my wife and I struggled financially to make ends meet. Since then, I made it my business to learn the skills and financial knowledge to start and achieve financial independence. After 12 years of learning, applying, and trial and error, I am on the journey to financial freedom. If you lose control of your finances at this moment, it is not too late. This book is your chance to start over financially and change your life forever. It took me 12 years to put together all the concepts that I have been learning and practicing in this practical book "Manage Your Money and Master Your Life" to help others to start and continue on their financial freedom journey.

Before the 2008 crisis, I relied on my job (my only source of income) to take care of my family. I thought that my job would be providing all the money I needed and more, no matter what I spent. Boy, was I wrong. I spent all my income on things that were not important. I did not have a reserve or invest for the future. My wife and I were financially unprepared to handle the difficult times during the 2008 economic crisis. Due to this, after 2008, we had changed our mindset about money, spending, investing, and financial freedom. It is my purpose to help as many people as possible to join us in the journey to financial freedom.

I have read hundreds of books and have been to many investment training sessions. But I could not find a single practical book that could help me implement the skills right away without buying expensive mentorship programs. After paying thousands of dollars in real estate investment training and taking many classes in financial investment and management, I finally put together this practical book with you and my family in mind. This book is also a reference for my kids to apply in their own financial life. I have written and prepared this collection of principles to share with you and guide you through the steps you need to take in order to achieve your financial freedom. I could remember, as clear as today, all my mother's advice about saving money for rainy days and investing in land. But it was too late for me to implement this into my life, as I was already in deep trouble in 2008. My mother, Jesula Julien, was an entrepreneur and she believed in financial freedom. She always taught all her 8 kids about money. I want to start this book off with 3 significant pieces of advice from my mother

* *Mindset;* money is important in this life and we need to learn about it.

* *Discipline;* success depends on your discipline. It is the requirement for financial success.

* *Planning;* you should always have an implementation plan for your money and your future.

The book is divided into 4 parts. The first part is about mindset, discipline, and planning. The first 2 chapters of the first part are dealing with the mindset for building wealth. Everything starts with a thought; you must get your mind ready for money, discipline your behavior to start using good money-handling habits, and constantly adjust your plans as you move forward and advance. The other 3 parts of the book are dedicated to the 10 practical lessons and concepts that you need to implement in your finances as you go through the book. Part 2 is about your current cash position and how to increase your income, control your expenses, and increase your cash. Part 3 will help you to focus on your financial position. Your financial position helps you increase what you own, and decrease or get rid of what you owe. The last part of the book focuses on buying power, credit, and real-life examples to help you apply the lessons and concepts.

I welcome you to the beginning of this journey to financial freedom. It is important to take time to read each chapter as many times as possible before moving to the next chapter. Also, I advise you to practice each lesson and concept in your finances as you move along each chapter. Each chapter contains a model and an example to help you implement what you learn in the chapter. I believe that, if you follow the book and apply the lessons and concepts step by step, you can turn your life around and improve your financial life, all for the better.

Sezair Julien

Part One

Mindset, Discipline, and Planning

Chapter 1

Mindset for Building Wealth

"Wisdom is a shelter as money is a shelter, but the advantage of knowledge is this: that wisdom preserves the life of its possessor." -Ecclesiastes 7:12

It is important to have a positive and educated mindset for building wealth. I want to take a moment to talk about why we need to train ourselves and teach our kids about money. Money is the currency of this world. After our spiritual life, money is one of the important things to learn to manage, because the quality of life under the sun depends on it. After losing my job and security in 2008, I realized the importance of having money to pay for daily necessities. I started to understand that struggling people think about money differently than wealthy people do. I had to change my mindset about wealth and learn how to create, build, and manage it.

When learning and reading about money and wealth, I could not grasp why they wouldn't teach us about money and how it works at school. In my personal study, money has become my most favored subject. The way that we think about money and the emotion we attach to it will be different when we know what money is and how money works. A lot of people think there is a conspiracy of the rich to keep the subject of money and basic finance out of the school system. I learned that money is exchange, money is a servant, not a master; money is anything of value, money is an idea, and we can all create money. I had always previously thought and heard from others that the poor were struggling because of the rich. I was surprised when I read in the bible that God created all people, and some decide to be rich and others decide to be poor. But now I realize we all have the same opportunities to create and build wealth. We need to start learning about money concepts and apply them to our financial life. After you finish reading and studying this book, you will see and know what I am talking about. Focus on and pay close attention to thought, mindset, and emotion about money going forward. Your financial education will become your number two priority after your spiritual life. Let us look at the three important things about our mindset for building wealth.

The first important thing about mindset for building wealth is:

Mindset Conditioning for Wealth

First, we need to change our mindset about money. We should not leave our financial life to someone else to take care of for us. We must build our economic life with careful planning and great intention. Much like a builder creating a design to build a house, your financial or economic life must be created. It is not something that just happens. We must maintain our wealth after we acquire it. We cannot maintain what we do not understand and plan for. Secondly, we must know that everything starts in the mind. Our financial mindset is one of the most important conditions that can transform our life and the life of our families.

We must not associate negativity with money and wealth. Most people associate negative emotion with money, but they still want and need it. They spend their lives working for it. We need to start focusing on our mindset and mental attitude about money and wealth. We must look at money for what it is and for all the positive things it can do for us. Let me say this once and for all: it is okay to have money and a lot of it."

What can we do to start conditioning our mind to build, create, and maintain wealth?

We must agree that having an abundance or surplus of money is okay. You must decide a specific amount of money that is abundant for you and make it your goal. It should exceed our necessities. You should strive to multiply your income to create a surplus in your finances.

We must develop an effective strategy on how to build our wealth and our family's wealth. We must think about how to make our money work for us. It all starts in the mind. Let us look at how to make our money produce more money for us.

First, we need to fix our mind on successful thought and act on successful processes. Here are 3 simple things anyone can do:

1) Model successful people and practice true principles. What do successful people do? Hear what Jesus of Nazareth said about practicing truth: *"Then you will know the truth, and the truth will set you free."* You will only be free when you know the truth (mind) and practice what you know (doing).

2) Create your process of creating wealth by developing a plan and using the right vehicle. The plan begins as a mental plan. Once you put it down on paper, it starts to become your goal. You continue to break it down to manageable steps that you can do every day.

3) Follow your plan religiously. The practice part is the hardest part to master because these principles are not your habits yet. You need to repeat them many times, so they will become part of your subconscious and second nature to you.

Second, practice makes you better every day. You must follow through and implement all of these steps into your life; doing is more important than just knowing.

You must continue making small steps toward your goal and your plan. Even though the steps of your plan become your goals, they must be S.M.A.R.T (specific, measurable, achievable, reliable, and timely). Here are a couple questions to keep in mind:

Is there a specific amount you have in mind that you are committed to? Is this plan achievable by you or someone else? How do you know that you are achieving it? What is your strategy to get there? When do you plan to get there?

And last, once we have S.M.A.R.T goals as part of our plan, we need to practice them every day until they become ingrained in our subconscious, our thought center. Your goal becomes your guiding step toward the goals that you set for yourselves. If you continue this path, you will accomplish your plan. I believe this simple mental model of making money can work for anyone and can be applied to any goal that someone might have.

The second important thing in our mindset for building wealth is:

The Way We Think About Money
Most of us have been conditioned to think negatively about money and wealth. We learn about money and wealth from people who have never built wealth. People always say:

* Money is the root of all evil
* People born rich
* Rich people will not go to heaven
* Rich people will always be rich and poor people will always be poor

Now, I have learned that these sayings are nothing but lies that struggling people have been telling themselves instead of learning how to create wealth and become rich. We all have the same 24 hours and breathe the same air. We all can decide any day to start changing our lives. In my Haitian culture, some people believe rich people get their wealth from the devil. These monetary beliefs prevent us from getting, building, and creating wealth. We need to change this mindset and think differently about money and wealth. It took me a long time to train my mind to change my thinking about money and wealth. This book presents a practical way to do so and start anyone on a path to build wealth. Money is nothing but value. Anything of value that we own is money.

Everyone should read "Think and Grow Rich" by Napoleon Hill. Here are 7 mind-changing principles that you can learn and practice every day from Napoleon Hill to start your life changing wealth building process and strategy:

1) Thoughts become things. Steve Job says "Everything around you that you call life was made up by people who were not smarter than you. And you can change it, you can influence it, you can build your own things that other people can use." If we understand that, money is an idea. Wealth is ideas becoming things. Money is ideas becoming things. When people use them, they give them value. God designed the universe in his mind first before he started creating it. We should not forget that we are created in God's image and likeness. Our thinking holds the key to money and wealth.

2) We must have the burning desire to see our ideas (our dream) become realities or things. Hill said, "The starting point of all riches is a burning desire for them. This is the emotional fuel that drives people to success."

We will not change what we tolerate. If we tolerate poverty and luck, we will never gain wealth. If we tolerate abuse, we will be abused by others. Until we make our mind up and have a burning desire to change our position, nothing will change for us. We must become sick and tired of our situation to change our mind about it. Then, we can change our lives.

3) We must set a definite goal to bring our thoughtful plan to life.

Most people have a lot of wishes for money, wealth, power, fame, and limitless ability. They want an easy life and social recognition, but many of these people do not have a definite plan to achieve them.

Hill reminds us "riches do not respond to wishes. They only respond to clear and definite goals." Here is what you can start doing:

1) First, be clear on where you are going.
2) Second, create a plan (steps) to show how you are going to get there.
3) You might get off track by life, but make this your second main goal.
4) Take immediate steps towards correct behavior and adjust your plan as necessary.
5) Decide exactly what you will give in return for this goal.
6) Action, action, action.

4) Be persistent because adversity will come.

Overcoming obstacles and getting past roadblocks are part of your journey. Most people fail because of the habit of quitting when temporary defeat shows up. A few will keep going despite adversity and bad luck. Challenges, defeats, and problems are temporary, and they come as a sign to teach us how to revise and adjust our plans to make them robust. Every successful person will tell you that they only became successful after bankruptcy or after they got past the point of quitting.

We need to remember that persistence is a signpost in the life story of every successful person. In the pursuit of wealth, it is no different. We need to be persistent. Do not quit.

5) Do not fear the critics.

Criticism is a powerful force that affects most of us. Criticism can make people hopeless and depressed. Sometimes it can come from people close to us like family and friends. We can all recall being bullied as a child in our youth. It is very demoralizing. We must protect ourselves against these negative influences. We must practice habits of keeping busy with our definite purpose, plans and results.

Also, mind control is the result of self-discipline and good habits. We must control our mind and our habits, or it will control us and our destinations.

6) Reject all excuses from yourself and others.

People who are not successful always have many excuses. If you pay more attention to their words, you'll find that they have created beliefs and stories to explain their own lack of achievement. They always start with these excuses:

* If only I was younger…

* If I was not married…

* If I had more money…

* If I was born rich…

* If the economy was better…

* If a democrat was in power…

* If I had good health…

* If I was lucky…

We need to recognize that every human being has the same 24 hours a day.

Let me repeat this bible proverb: *"God creates all people, some become rich and others become poor,"* proverb 22, verse 2.

We must not give excuses; we should instead spend more time analyzing our weaknesses and failures in order to transform them into strengths and learning opportunities. They become adjustments to achieve more success tomorrow. Our limitations are sometimes exactly what we need to start a revolution in our mind. Limitations are opportunities in reverse, and we need to use them for our advancement in life.

7) Develop your specialized knowledge to put into action.

We do not get paid because we have a lot of knowledge, we get paid by the problems we solve for others. The right knowledge organized and applied to solve real problems is what makes people successful. We need to start immediately with our financial education, and we need to have started studying wealth yesterday.

The third important thing in our mindset for building wealth is our financial education.

Financial Education
Financial freedom is based on our self-education. It is important because it gives us the ability to understand

money, but also it teaches us how to manage and create assets, which are wealth.

Real wealth is portable and transferable. The most portable wealth in life is knowledge. Once you have knowledge, nobody can take it away from you. People say knowledge is power, but it is also very important to put this knowledge to use; this is where the real power is. We must put our knowledge to use if we want to see the fruit of it. Knowledge is like seeds. We will see the power of a seed when we plant it. Seed becomes a tree and produces more fruits. We must practice what we know. The best part is that you can transfer your financial education to your family members, friends, community, and the world. Let us look at the difference between classical education and financial education.

Classical and Professional Education

Classical and professional education teaches us how to read, write, and how to gain knowledge. It also teaches us how to work for someone all our lives. It trains us to think like employees. This advice includes studying hard, having good grades, and having a good job that you are satisfied with and pays well. With this system, you guarantee to work all your life for a company, and they will contribute to your 401k (retirement plan) if you contribute some amount. You will buy a home, a couple of cars, have credit card debts, and have a few kids. In other words, the corporations in the capitalist system will own you like plantation owners owned their slaves. They will determine your worth, how much money you make, and where you live. This is every American's dream. In this system, you pay everyone first after you receive your paycheck, and you pay yourself last if anything is left. You become the slave and loser. Some people call this system "the rat race." That means, at the end of the month or year, you are in the same position you were from the start.

We must start our financial education early on in order to help us manage, invest, and multiply our income. Financial education is the only way out of this rat race that most of us are in. Going to college to get a professional education is not enough anymore. Vocational school, community and 4-year college are designed to train employees. Even though professional education is important and a good way to start acquiring income (money) for most of us, financial education is the knowledge and wisdom that can put us on the journey to financial freedom. Neither classic nor professional education teach us about money, despite money being a center of real life. I must make this clear: we need both classic and professional education, they help us to increase our earning potential. But financial education is required to achieve financial freedom. It is a long-term journey that should start in middle school and continue until death. Financial education focuses on investing, multiplying, managing, and saving money for our current life, our family life, and for generations to come. We need to continue asking ourselves "How should we use our current income to achieve financial freedom?" It is the question that financial education answers. Financial literacy should start in middle school and continue in high school, through college, and beyond. Personal financial investing and management should be a requirement in all colleges. As you continue to read and practice what is in this practical book, you will start on your own journey to financial freedom. I believe your life will never be the same.

**keep reading **

Chapter 2

DISCIPLINE AND A FINANCIAL PLAN

"Discipline is the bridge between thought and accomplishment."-Jim Rohn

Looking back to 2008 with my lack of financial education, I was on a destructive path of spending my wealth. Not just me; some of my family members were on the same course that I was on. During the 2008 crisis, some of them lost their houses because of a lack of reserve, savings, and investment for tomorrow. I come from a big family, and I am the youngest of 8. Even though my mother always talked to us about a life of discipline and to always have a plan, we forgot to practice what we learned from our entrepreneur mother until we were deep in trouble. I have been working on my financial education to avoid being in the same position again. Since then, I have been practicing strict discipline with my finances and my personal life. I have a plan for every penny that I earn.

I have learned that discipline only works if we have a reason for it. Discipline with no result in mind is almost practically impossible. Many people make that mistake every day. I used to talk to my kids about living a life of discipline. But I never showed them a picture of why they need to be disciplined. We took a walk, my kids and I, through the worst neighborhood in our city and then took them to my hometown-village in Haiti. They got the picture of why they had to be disciplined. They do not want to live in a bad neighborhood. Being financially independent becomes the focus of my life and my family's life. Then, my wife and I can start helping our kids develop a plan for their future. Things become easier. When you know a life of freedom for the rest of your life is the picture to be accomplished, discipline becomes achievable. Do you want to be financially free? Then you must start on your financial discipline and plan. I also believe that planning is nothing but your map to get from where you are to where you want to go financially in life. I used to be intimidated by goal-setting and planning for the long term because I did not have the money to achieve the goals. Now, I learned that your goals bring you the result that you are looking for. There is a little Haitian proverb that goes "Little by little, a bird makes its nest." I believe goal-setting and planning is that way. The big goal is to build a financial nest and the plan is to do it one day at a time.

I don't know about you, but I was a Mr. Right Now. Back then, I wanted to drive the best car and live in the best neighborhood, which is fine. The only problem was that my money was not enough to live like the Joneses. I did not understand why delayed gratification was important. I thought I must work 24/7 to keep up a lifestyle of showing off to people that I did not even like. What a crazy way to live! After dedicating my whole life to financial freedom, I understood that I had to delay short term pleasure for a long term of happiness. Discipline, like we talked of earlier, is the basis of delaying your gratification now for learning how to create many sources of income for a better tomorrow. I invite you to take the time to carefully review discipline, delay gratification, and planning before we dive into the 10 concepts that will change your life starting in part 2 of the book.

What is discipline?

Discipline: training that corrects, molds or perfects. The mental faculties or moral character.-Merriam-Webster

Discipline from Latin. "Disco," the process by which one learns a way of life.- light.org

Discipline is a way of life. Financial discipline is being in control of our money; it is the ability to control our spending habits, save our money and invest according to the plan that we want to achieve.

Each person needs to be able to apply these definitions of discipline to his or her life at some level. This is where self-discipline comes in.

What is self-discipline?

Self-discipline is the individual ability of a person to control his or her internal impulse to not react to external stimuli. It is also the drive to accomplish self-imposed goals even when the external situation of life is going the opposite way.

Self-discipline is a standard imposed by self on an area of life to attain a certain goal. Financial discipline is self-imposed financial standard (goals) in order to change from luck to abundance or from poverty to financial freedom.

Self-discipline is a necessity if we want to achieve financial freedom. Everyone is trying to get money from the landlord, lenders, credit cards, and investment bank for entertainment. Television has bombarded us with commercials that attract or entice us to buy everything under the sun. In order to set a financial path for our family, we must have discipline.

The Importance of Financial Discipline.

Self-discipline is key to success and makes you aware of what you don't need or what you are doing is going to negatively affect your goals. Financial discipline gives you the ability to control your expenses, to build your assets, to reduce your liabilities and to focus on the future. Financial discipline provides a whole new view and direction of your life and can help us build a steady financial base for our family.

Financial discipline will allow us to achieve financial freedom for us and generations to come. As we develop self-discipline for a successful financial life, we must ignore or fight anything in life that could keep us from achieving our goal. Discipline helps us understand and use delayed gratification to our advantage

What is Delayed Gratification?
"Rule your mind or it will rule you." – Horace

Delayed gratification is the act of resisting an impulse to take an immediately available reward in hopes of obtaining a more valuable reward in the future. It is essential to self-regulation or self-control"-Britannica online

Back in 200 BC, Aristotle saw people were not happy because they confused pleasure (short term) for true happiness (long term). According to Aristotle, true happiness is the discipline to develop long term habits. They will help you to move toward your greatest potential.

I would say that delayed financial gratification, then, is the discipline of delaying the pleasure of having things that will lose value in order to acquire a long-term asset that will produce a return for a lifetime. Delayed gratification requires discipline, time management, and patience to achieve.

Benefits of Financial Delayed gratification
There are many advantages and benefits to financial delayed gratification. We will look at 3 benefits:

1) Financial delayed gratification helps us be more aware of short-term pleasures of buying things that we do not need in order to invest the money for our long-term security and enjoyment. For example, instead of taking a loan to buy a new

car, you can buy a used car cash and invest the rest of your money in a company that pays a dividend.

2) Financial delayed gratification helps us see and understand the financial reward of investing for the long term or for the future. For example, instead of buying a boat, you can buy an investment duplex that will produce income for the rest of your life.

3) 3- Financial delayed gratification is essential; you must learn to delay unnecessary purchases if you want to build wealth to pass on to your descendants or to future generations. I love what Solomon says in proverb 13, verse 22:

"A good person leaves an inheritance for their children's children."

We have the responsibility to build wealth for our future, our children, and our children's children. We will be able to do that when we start delaying urges in order to build wealth for the long term. We can start a 529 plan for our grandkids instead of buying them toys and gifts. You can start a retirement plan for your grandkids now that can grow for the next 60 years with an 8% return in the market.

Creation of a Financial Plan
"Prepare your work outside; get everything ready for yourself in the field, and after that build your house."- Proverbs 24:27

Just like how the proverb says to get ready, you must build your plan of action. After you build your investment or your field, then you go home and rest. You do not rest until you are done. During creation, God only rests when he is done with everything. We need to learn planning or financial planning from the master Himself.

A financial plan is a blueprint or a map of our financial life; it helps us recognize and establish our financial goals, what our current position is, our destination and where we want to be, and how to get there. If we follow our financial plan, we will know how to use, manage, and invest our money wisely to accomplish our financial goals.

To create a simple financial plan that anyone can follow and implement, we will go over one example. It will have 2 parts to it: the financial goals and financial strategies.

First, we need to learn how to set our financial goals.

"Goals without reason will fail"

a) **Write down what you value in life**. In other words, what is your purpose? What drives you? What are you passionate about? This is the "why" part of your goals. Also known as the most significant part of your journey.

   For example, I have 3 main values for my life and my family:

   1) My freedom (going and doing what I want and when I want)
   2) My family's well-being (paying for my kids' college education and setting up a legacy for the next generations)
   3) Giving (contributing to my local church, community and helping others)

   Take some time to write down your goals by starting with your values (or your "why").

b) **Derive your financial goals from your values or your why**.

   Write down the goals that will help you live your values every day.

   1) For example, I will need to produce 6k/

month from my investments to be financially free.

2) I need a surplus of 2k to invest towards my kids' education and to leave a legacy.

3) I need to be able to give $500 a month.

I need 10k a month to achieve my financial freedom.

*As you can see, my financial goals are connected to my values. This is important because most people give up because they do not have a reason big enough that can make them change their financial behavior. Go ahead and write down your goals now.

c) **Break down your goals into achievable steps that can become habits in your life**.

For example:

1) Saving $150 a week for one year (52 weeks) will give you $7,800.00

If you continue to save $150 per week for two years, you can accumulate $15,600. You can put that money down on an investment home that can produce $400 to $600 in cash flow every month, for a total of $7,000 a year. What if you have the ability to acquire 15 to 20 properties in the next 20 years of your working life? You will be able to have an income of $120k to $140k a year without counting your income from your job. Can $140,000.00/year be enough for your retirement? How much money do you need to produce to replace your job? It is up to you to figure this out.

2) The mortgage for the 20 income properties will be paid off by the tenants in 30 years. After paying the mortgages, your 20 income-

producing properties can bring $30,000.00 to $40,000.00 per month with a $2,000.00 per month, per property, for a total of $360,000.00 to $480,0000.00 per year. You can retire anytime you want. Anyone can do that, and you do not need a college degree to do that.

3) Your legacy and family's well-being are all set, and you will be able to give with pleasure like God wants you to. We need to start thinking about our financial life right now.

d) **One other important step in our goal setting should be taking a class, seminar, or reading a financial book every month, at least**.

Set your financial education process in motion, like this book indicates. You cannot create, build, protect, and pass your wealth down to the next generation without financial education.

e) **Teach financial freedom principles to your children and grandchildren and great-grandchildren**.

This happens a lot where someone spends a lifetime building wealth and their kids destroy the legacy in less than 5 years. They do not leave anything or grow it and pass it on to other generations. Educate your kids financially. School does not teach financial literacy.

f) **The last step in your plan is to build a team of professionals in your corner**.

You need a team of:

* Lawyers

* Personal trainers

* Real estate professionals

* Estate planners

* Financial advisors

You can add anyone that you need to your team. Most of the services for these professionals are free anyway. They will be happy to teach you about how the financial system works and how life works. Make sure you pay your team well, so you can get the best advice.

If you have not closed the book so far, you are the exact person I had in mind when I decided to write this book. Go to the next section to start with the financial skills required for your financial freedom.

Part Two

Cash Position
(Where is your money?)

The 10 financial terms or concepts that can change your life forever

Chapter 3

INCOME STATEMENT
(Position of Cash Flow)

Financial term or Concept 1: Income statement or profit / loss statement

"The minute a Wall Street firm purchases your debt, your bank no longer has it on its financial statement, which then allows the bank to look for more credit card customers. That's one reason why you get so many credit card offers." Robert Kiyosaki

As we dive into the 10 financial concepts that I believe everyone should understand and practice, your life is about to change forever. As I am writing this book, we are in the middle of a health crisis (Covid-19), which then created an economic crisis. During this economic crisis, there is a great transfer of wealth happening at the same time. People who are financially educated are making a killing in the stock market, but the rest of the population are losing 20 to 35% of their retirement money in 401k. I remember, in 2008, the same thing happened to me. Due to my understanding of the 10 financial concepts I am teaching you, my economic struggles have been reversed. Today in 2020, stocks are at their lowest since 2008. As more people pull away from the stock market, others with a financial education are going in. Don't you think you should be part of the 5% who make money during a crisis? Educating yourself financially is the first and most important step in your journey. This book is doing exactly that for you. These 10 financial concepts are not only applied to your personal finance, but they are the fundamentals of all investments, businesses, and governments. We cannot afford to not understand and use financial statements in our everyday financial life.

The first time I learned about financial statements, such as income statements, I was upset that nobody ever spoke to me about basic principles of finance. Back in 2008, I had been in the labor market for over 10 years. I have an associate degree and bachelor's degree in engineering, yet I had never heard about income statements and how to use them in my financial life. I did not even understand what my cash position meant. I was educated, but I was financially illiterate. I was convinced right away that I had to turn my life around and start learning finance if I wanted to become successful. By reading this book, you are on your way to strengthen your financial muscle and improve your life considerably.

The rich have studied, mastered, and used these concepts and principles since the beginning of time. I understand now why I was poor even though I was making a decent income from my job. The wealthy teach their kids these principles at the dinner table and behind closed doors, but the struggling have no idea that there is a process to making money and getting rich. You are about to get your revelation about money. Remember like anything else: it is the application of these principles that will make you rich and lead to success and long-term enjoyment. If you just read the book and not apply the concepts in the book, you will be in the same position when I release the next book that will take you over to financial freedom. You should study, practice, and teach these principles to your kids from middle school until they master their own financial lives.

We will start part 2 of the book with the 3 chapters on Income statement, beginning with income, expenses, and cash flow. I want you to pay close attention, even if you might have heard these terms before. I believe these concepts are so simple and easy to understand, but their application can be extremely hard to implement into your life. That is why only 1 to 5% of people are rich and successful when it comes to money.

What is an Income Statement? What is your cash position?

The income statement or profit/loss statement is the record of all money coming in to your pocket and all money going out of your pocket. It gives you a picture of your cash position at the end of the month, quarter, or year. Your income statement can be compared to your health checkup. When you go to your doctor for your monthly, quarter, and annual checkup, he or she gives you a report of your health position, in terms of blood pressure, BMI, and blood sugar. With this health position, you know if you need to continue on your path or if you need to change direction. If your blood pressure is good, your blood sugar is well-controlled, and your body mass index is under the limit, the doctor tells you congratulations and continues your path of healthy living. However, if the indicators are beyond the limits, the doctor would highly recommend changing your path, or your living style. It is the same way for your financial checkup. Your financial wealth is in your hands, and you must take action. Knowledge without action will not give you results. You are about to compare your health checkup with your first wealth checkup:

First Financial Checkup			
Health Checkup		Wealth Checkup	
Health statement		Income Statement	
Blood pressure		Income	
Blood sugar		Expenses	
BMI		Cash flow	

Like the health checkup, the income statement is your first financial checkup. It reveals your income, expenses, and your cash flow. This is known as your cash position. How much cash is coming in? How much cash do you burn every month? How much do you have left? Do you see how important that is? You become your own doctor by reading and applying the principles in this book.

Why do you need to understand your income statement?

The income statement gives you your cash position at the end of the month, quarter, and year. It also shows if you are getting yourself into debt by spending more of your income than you are receiving. It will tell you if you are poor or rich when it comes to cash. It shows you the flow of your cash. If you are serious about financial independence, it is the most important thing you need to understand to be able to create more income and to control your money. Your money flow in your life is like the flow of blood in your body. You do not want to have less of it; it is like committing slow suicide or experiencing a slow death. If you have more of it, you can give some away. That is the position we all want to be in.

At the end of every week/month, you should be able to know if you are running or operating on a deficit (loss) or a profit (benefit). In other words, you need to know if you have cash left or if you need more cash for your debts and expenses. In comparison to the body, if you do not have blood you are dead. Life is in the blood. If you do not have cash or operate in the positive (profit) or spend more than your income, you are bankrupt or financially dead.

The income statement or profit/loss statement has 3 main blocks or parts: your income, your expenses, and cash flow or cash position. Use this model to practice as we go.

MODEL OF INCOME STATEMENT

INCOME		
Earned Income		Amount
	Earned #1	
	Earned #2	
	Earned Total	
Passive Income		
	Real Estate (Net)	
	Business (Net)	
	Passive Total	
Portfolio Income		
	Interest	
	Dividends	
	Royalties	
	Portfolio Total	
TOTAL MONTHLY INCOME		

EXPENSES

TAXES		LIVING EXPENSES		LUXURY EXPENSES	
NAME	**AMNT**	**EXPENSE NAME**	**AMNT**	**EXPENSE NAME**	**AMNT**
STATE		Taxes (Real Estate)		Boat	
Medicare		Home Mortgage (insurance)		Designer bags	
Medicaid		Utilities (Electric, Gas, Water, sewer, cable)		Lot of toys for kids	
		Maintenance		Cars	
401K		Insurance (car)		Expensive watches	

		Food and Clothing		expensive vacations	
		Other Expenses (gas for cars)		Credit card 2	
		Tithing/ Donation			
		Credit Card #1			
		Car Loan #1			
		student Loan #1			
		personal Loan #1			
		Phones			
Total Taxes	**$** -	**TOTAL LIVING EXPENSES**	**$** -	**TOTAL LUXURY EXP.**	**$** -
TOTAL EXPENSES			**$**	-	

NET INCOME OR CASH FLOW	
	AMOUNT
Total Income	
Total Expenses	
INCOME – EXPENSES	
NET CASH FLOW	

Everyone should prepare their income statement. Now you have been educated on income statements but, before going into detail on expenses, income, and net income or cash flow, you should use the model of income statement to begin on your own income statement. Take the time to start filling out your detailed income statement to find out your cash position right now before you move on to the next concept or chapter. Do not delay this practical step. That is the most important part of the book.

Principles learned that you need to practice

* *Your income statement is like your health checkup. It reveals your financial wellbeing.*

* *Income statements are used by financial institutions like lenders and banks to analyze your cash position.*

* *The income statement or profit/loss statement is the record of all money coming into your pocket and all money going out of your pocket.*

Now that we know our position of cash or income statement, we can move on to learning about ways to increase our income and make more money.

Chapter 4

INCOME
(Many ways to make money)

Financial term or concept 2: Our income

"The goal of retirement is to live off your assets-not on them." - Frank Eberhart

I have been trained to study hard, have good grades, resulting in a good job ever since I started school a long time ago. My mother, who was an entrepreneur, did not formally teach me about entrepreneurial skills and how to start a business. To her credit, she always taught me to invest and take good care of my money. It never dawned on me that there are many types of incomes. After I moved to the United States of America, I thought income and money would come from a good job through a college degree. I later found out that there are many sources of money or income. Money is the reward for the service and product that we render to other people. Here are some definitions of money:

"Money is your intellectual capacity."

"Money is your idea."

"Money is your product."

"Money is your service."

"Money is material."

"Money is resources, etc."

My point is anything can become money. You need to focus on every possible resource of money when you are looking at your income and all potential income sources. When I realized anything with value can become a source of income, I was financially free. The financial freedom that we are looking for starts in our mind. We should never forget that. I can remember my first business at the end of 2008 was a 50 square feet shoe store at the Laurel, Delaware flea market. I would go to Manhattan, New York to buy shoes for about $15 to $20 a pair, and I would sell them for $40 to $50 dollars a pair. Looking back at it, it was a very profitable small business. One day, I saw an interview with Demon John that changed my life. He was explaining how he got started selling shoes in his bedroom. I was not afraid anymore of what people would say about me selling shoes at a flea market as a college graduate. The next day, I started selling shoes on eBay as well. I learned more about business in the flea market than I learned during my Master of Science in management 3 years later. At the flea market, I started learning about income, expenses, and cash flow. As you are going through the income chapter, you need to start thinking about other sources of potential income that you can start developing. Let us look at the definition of income.

What is income?

1) Income is the amount of money or equivalent received in exchange for labor or services, from sale of goods or property or as a profit from investment.-American heritage

2) Income is money received on a regular basis, for work or through investments.-The Finish Rich Dictionary by David Bach.

3) My definition is even simpler:

All money that is coming into our pocket or bank account or to us in the form of cash, check, and value is considered income.

These definitions tell us where the money is coming

from and how we get it. Let us look at the income model in detail. There are 3 types of regular income per our example above. I would go further to say that there are 4 types of income: active, positive, business, and donation.

TYPE OF INCOME

INCOME		
Earned Income		**Amount**
	Earned #1	
	Earned #2	
	Earned Total	
Passive Income		
	Real Estate	
	Business	
	Passive Total	
Portfolio Income		
	Interest	
	Dividends	
	Royalties	
	Portfolio Total	
TOTAL MONTHLY INCOME		

Active Income

By selling your time, you receive active income. We need to understand time is the main factor in active income. If you do not go to work, you do not have an income or money. People call selling time new slavery, merry go round, and "rat race." You probably heard these terms before. Here is how the rate race cycle goes:

Rate race or merry go round cycle of selling time for money

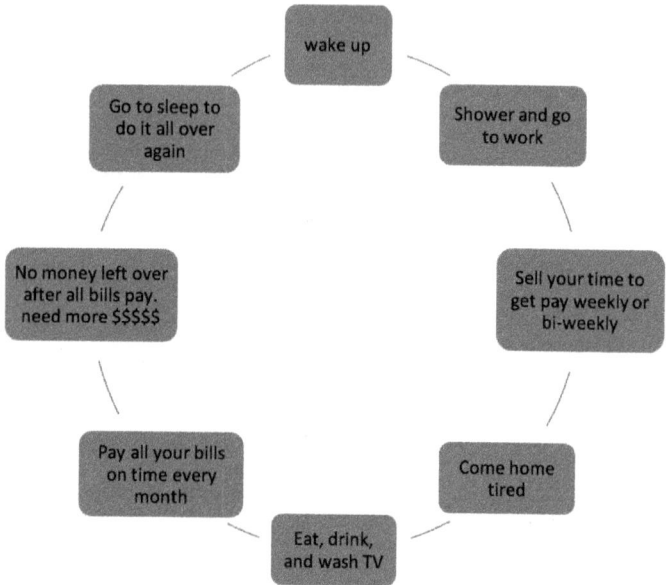

Life becomes a never-ending cycle until retirement, broke, and death.

Does this cycle represent your everyday life? If it is, this book will open your eyes to other possibilities for a better financial life. Time is literally money for those who are living in the rat race. It does not matter if you are working at McDonald's or if you are working as a doctor. At the end of the day, you are selling your time for money. If you stop going to work and are not physically present, you stop making money. This is a big problem. We need to learn to leverage our capital, people, and material to produce incomes. I will coach you there.

The active income is fine if you learn how to manage your money. This is what this book is all about. Your work might be your passion in life, but you need money to live in this world. We spend hours in our job, but we still live paycheck by paycheck. We need to do something different. What I am saying is that we need to pay attention and learn how the money game works. I think David Bach says it best: "What matters from now on is to finish rich." So we can finish rich, live comfortably, and enjoy life with our money. No matter what, it should be your choice whether or not you want to work for a company. We can work while our money is working for us also.

We must point out that some people only have one way to make money: get a job, get another job on top of their original job, or work more overtime. There are many other ways to create or make money. We need to educate ourselves on all possibilities to create income if we want to achieve financial freedom.

Passive Income

Passive income is money received from your investment on a regular basis. Personally, I love passive income because there is no need for me to sell my time in order to receive an income. It is coming every week or month, or quarterly, or yearly even if I do not do anything. When our passive income is more than our expenses, then we are free. Let us look at some examples of passive income:

Example 1: Passive Income: Rental Property

Duplex Purchase Information

Purchase Price:	$	100,000.00
Bankloan:	$	90,000.00
Your down payment:	$	10,000.00
Closing cost:	$	6,000.00
Appraisal and inspection:	$	1,000.00
Insurance:	$	1,200.00
Total Cost to you:	**$**	**18,200.00**

Duplex income(2 tenants at $1000.00 each)

Monthly Income:	+$	2,000.00
Mortgage (tax+insrnce):	-$	950.00
Maintenance:	-$	$100.00
Water & sewer:	-$	250.00
Vacancy:	-$	100.00
Reserve:	-$	100.00
Total monthly expenses:	**-$**	**1,500.00**

Total monthly Income (net cash flow): + $500.00

As long as we can delay our gratification and discipline ourselves, we can save up money in order to buy passive income. In this example, we can save $20k in 2 to 3 years to buy a duplex which can bring us $500 a month and $6000 a year for the next 30 years for a total of $180,000.00. The best part is the tenants are paying for the mortgage, so we do not have to do anything. After that 30 years, you will receive $2000.00 a month and $24,000.00 a year until you die. Here is the best part: you will pass it down to the next generations. What if you can buy 10 duplexes? Imagine that...

Example 2: Stocks (passive and portfolio)

Company XYZ is selling for $2 a share

Pay Dividend: .20 cents per quarter

After your financial and technical analysis, you decide to buy 150 stocks/shares for $300.

Case 1 (share of XYZ decrease to $1.50)

Time frame (month)	3
Number of shares of XYZ	150
price per share	$ 1.50
Dividend	$ 0.10
Total Cost	$ 300.00
Quarterly dividend payment	$ 15.00

yearly	$ 60.00
Return	20%
portfolio value	$ 225.00

In case 1, the stock of XYZ company goes down to $1.50 per share. In that case, the company has decided to pay a dividend even though the stock is down. The business is very successful and bringing in good income. The stock is down because of trading, not because the company is not performing well. We still received 0.10 cents per share for a total of $15 in the first quarter. We are investing for the long term. We are not traders, but we are investors. It does not matter if the value of the stock is down by $0.50 cents and the value of the portfolio is down to $225.00. This is not our concern for the first quarter. We are not selling our position because the fundamentals of the company are strong. We still make a passive income of $15 that can compound to our portfolio to buy more stocks or we can decide to pay ourselves an income. I would advise buying more of the same stock since it becomes cheaper to own, and the cost to value decreased. The return and the dividend per cost increased, making us wealthier.

Case 2 (share of XYZ Increase to $6.0)

Time frame (months)	6
Number of shares of XYZ	150
price per share	$6
Dividend	0.20
total Cost	$ 300.00
Quarterly dividend payment	$ 30.00
yearly	$ 120.00
Return	40%
portfolio value	$ 900.00

In case 2, the stock of XYZ company increased to $6.00 per share. Because of the company's success, it pays a dividend of $0.20 per share. For the second quarter, we received a $30 dividend as passive income. The return for the quarter is 40% return on our cash. The value of our portfolio is increased to $900.00, and the portfolio is increased to 300%. Since we bought the company for the long term, we will continue to keep our stocks. If things are going according to plan, we are expected to get our money back in dividend payment in 2 ½ years or less because we can use the dividends to buy more shares and increase our quarterly income. Like Albert Einstein reputedly said,

" Compound interest is the eighth wonder of the world."

The best thing about this investment vehicle is that you do not have to do anything. Your dividend payment will continue to come to your bank account, so you can sleep all day. We need to learn to use part of our paycheck as capital to invest and buy companies that can increase our wealth.

Example 3: Write a book

Step 1:
You spend 6 months to a year writing a book. So far, you have not had a need to spend any money, but, instead, you have used your brain and knowledge. You spent your time to do your research and countless hours with your team to create your final manuscript.

Step 2:
You found a publisher that will publish, distribute, and market your book on their own expenses for a bigger return. You signed the contract for both a hardcover and eBook. You will receive $2.50 in royalty on each book sold at a price of $5.00 per book. This is a very conservative example because eBooks are selling for between $9.99 to $15.00, on average and hardcovers averaging between $12 to $19.

Step 3:
The publisher sets up the book tours and your speaking schedule. All you must do is go around and talk about your passion. Your time is your price up to this point because the publisher covers all your travel costs.

Step 4:
The book becomes a best seller with 25,0000

copies sold in the first month with a price of $5 per book. That will bring an income of $125,000.00 in the first month. In 6 months, you sold 100,000.00 copies for a total of $500,000.00. In less than 6 months, you can create an income revenue of $625,000. How is that for your mental stimulation?

Step 5:
You will continue to receive income for as long as you live every time a book is sold. This is a lifetime of income for you and your family.

Passive income is the reason Michael Jackson is richer dead than alive. His music continues to produce income for his family in royalties. That is why his family members are fighting for his legacy and his wealth. Michael Jackson continues to get paid for his music. That is amazing to me. The question for you and I is: can we do that? Of course.

Business or Portfolio Income

What is business or portfolio income?
Business or portfolio income is money received from a sale of goods and services of a business or sale of properties or stocks. It can also be the money received in a business after sales, interests, and payments are collected.

You must educate yourself on management and how to run a business if you want to create a business or be self-employed. The rest of this book is a great start because every concept we talked about applies to every kind of business.

Let us look at a couple examples of business or portfolio income:

Example 1: Flipping a property (buy, renovate, and sale a property)

Buy a single-family house for $140,000.00 to renovate and resell for a profit in 6 months:

Cost:

> Purchase Price: $140,000.00
> Down payment: $14,000.00
> Private Loan or Mortgage: $126,000.00
> Closing cost: $6,000.00
> Inspection: $500
> Appraisal: $500
> Total interest for 6 months mortgage: $5,400.00
> 6 months Property Tax: $2600.00

Total personal Cost: $29,000.00

Renovation cost: $25,000.00

Total Cost: $180,000.00

It took 4 months for the renovation and 2 months to sell the house.

Sale of Property: $210,000.00
Profit: $210,000.00 – $180,000.00 = $30,000.00
State and capital gain taxes: $6,500.00

Portfolio Net Profit: $ 23,500.00

What if we can learn to flip property as active portfolio income and turn the profit into passive income by buying rental properties? The possibilities might be endless! That is the reason I wrote this book; to teach others skills that can bring this financial expertise so anyone can achieve financial freedom .

Example 2: Sale of a product and service

Step 1: Open a service business (Ex. "ABC Lawn Care Services")

The company will provide residential lawn care around your town. There are 2 employees: The owner and one other employee. The entrepreneur used his credit card to spend $3,500 to start the company.

3 lawn mowers: $750.00
1 pickup truck: $2500.00
Supplies: $250.00

Step 2: services

Price: $60.00 per cut
30 yards per week
30 * 60 = $1800.00 a week

Step 3: financials

Monthly card payment: $200.00
Employee 1: $15.00 * 30 hours = $450.00
owner: $20.00 * 20 hours = $400.00
Gas and supplies: $100

Total expenses: $1150.00

Income: $60.00 * 30 = $1800.00
Net Income: $1800.00 – $1010.00 = $600.00

Taxes: $100.00

Real net weekly Income: $500.00

The portfolio income this small business can provide is $500 a week and $2,000 a month.. It does not take a lot to become an entrepreneur and create a business. What service can you offer to others that will give them value? A business is any entity that brings values to others. It can be a product or a service. People will pay for value. If you give people values, they will pay you money. Money is just an idea.

Donation Income

Donation income is money received from family, friends, and organization from the kindness of their hearts. Many people receive all their income by donation money alone. Some non-profit or charitable organizations' purposes are to provide help and care for the less fortunate in our society. They provide income to millions of people around the world like the Red Cross, World Foods, etc. This is great and we all should participate in providing income to these organizations.

Providers	Beneficiaries
Cities and charities population	Homeless
Moms and Dads and	College students
	kids
Families	Kids, cousins
Churches, charitable organizations	Refugees

Even though the classic financial does not include donation income as a type of income, it should still be included. Many people depend on giving or acts of charity for their money and income.

Now it is your time to practice filling out your income statement:

Income Of _____

Income =			
Active	**Passive**	**Portfolio**	**Donation**

Please add your name

Add all your types of income

Total all your income

Take time to review what we just covered before moving to the concept of expenses.

Principles that you need to practice

* *Money is the reward for the service and product that we render to other people.*

* *Money is your intellectual capacity. Money is your idea. Money is your product. Money is your service. Money is material. Money is resources.*

* *All money that is coming into your pocket or bank account or to you in the form of cash, check, and value is income.*

* *I would go further to say that there are 4 types of income: active, positive, business, and donation.*

* *We need to master the art of income creation if we want to achieve financial freedom.*

It is imperative after learning many ways to make money and 4 types of income to start creating more income for yourself. We will move to the financial concept that keeps most people from gaining wealth.

Chapter 5

Expenses
(Who controls your money)

Financial term or concept 3: Our Expenses

"Be aware of little expenses. A small leak will sink a great ship." - Benjamin Franklin

As I was starting to sell more shoes online and in the flea market, I realized that I must control my expenses. If I had to do it all over again from 21 years old to 30 years old, I would have controlled every penny I earned. We had spent every dollar my wife and I earned. This was very irresponsible, especially considering we had just started a family. Like Benjamin said, expenses can destroy your financial life little by little, like a small leak can sink a great ship, such as the Titanic. Sometimes, we don't realize how much debt we have gotten ourselves into or how much money we are paying others until we are no longer able to pay them. A debt-free lifestyle should be everyone's goal. Debt is the new form of slavery. Regardless of how much money we are making, we should never spend more than 70% of our net income. I recommend everyone to read "The Richest Man In Babylon." It is a small book that anyone can read in one sitting. In this book by Gorge S. Clason, the first thing you will learn is: "A part of all we learn is ours to keep." When it comes to expenses, I learned from that book that I need to control my expenditures. I learned to be able to identify the difference between my necessities and my desires. I was gratifying my desires with all my income. We all have more desires than necessities. We need to take care of our necessary expenses for our everyday living, and we need to control our desire and delay our gratification to build our wealth first. Let us look at expenses.

What are expenses?

According to the American Heritage Dictionary, expense is money, or something spent to accomplish a purpose. It is also charges incurred in the performance of work. It is something requiring the expenditure of money.

Expense is the cost required for something; the money spent on something per "The Finish Rich Dictionary."

Expense is all money going out of your pocket or bank account. It is all money paid out for anything.

Everyone has expenses, even if you do not have an income. The secret to financial freedom is to make, produce, or have more income than expenses. If we look at life on a financial basis, even babies and the deceased have expenses. In order to build our cash flow or net worth, we must learn to control all of our expenses. As we said in the previous chapter, discipline is the most important thing when it comes to control of expenses. We must have a plan or budget for every dollar we bring into our financial life.

There are three main categories of expenses: Taxes, Living, and Luxuries.

Type of Expenses

Expenses =		
Taxes	**Living**	**Luxuries**
Income taxes	Mortgage	Credit cards
Medicare/Medicaid	Bills	Cellphone
Property tax	Food/Clothes	Personal loan
Car tax	Student loans	

Taxes

Taxes are expenses that you must pay as contribution to your government (local/federal). We pay the government first when we are an employee. We need to learn to be entrepreneurs because they pay taxes last or at the end after all expenses paid. When you have an enterprise, you pay taxes on the profit only.

<u>Local taxes</u>: Property tax, car tax, sales tax

We pay these taxes ourselves. Property tax is used to pay for local government like school systems, snow removal, local police force, etc.

<u>State taxes</u>: Sales tax

State taxes are removed from every employee's paycheck by the employer. It is used for state government like roads, police force, etc. Sales tax is used for the same purpose as well, and you pay sales taxes when you purchase things.

<u>Federal taxes:</u> Federal taxes are taken from our paycheck by our employer. They are used by the federal government for services like highways, security, and the army.

<u>Medicare/Medicaid</u>: It is also taken from our paychecks for social services and medical services for the elderly.

If we do not pay enough taxes, we will pay the rest during income taxes, filling the first quarter of every year. Paying taxes is a good thing if they are used appropriately by our government. It is becoming a burden on the citizens when it becomes too high. The government is taking people's wealth through taxes by increasing taxes (government expenses). In order to keep the government small, we must keep our taxes under control. We can keep the government under control by voting for people that will keep the government small and businesses in charge of the economic system.

Living expenses

Living expenses are expenses that are required for everyday life. We all have them, whether we are working or not. If we let them out of our control, they can prevent us from achieving financial independence. We must use discipline to help us keep expenses under control. We are responsible for managing our money; we need to save, invest, and protect our money and wealth to last our lifetime and leave an inheritance of capital for our kids and grandkids. We need to start as early as possible and be responsible with our money.

Let us review an example of expenses. You can always add to the list for your specific case.

LIVING EXPENSES	
EXPENSE NAME	AMOUNT
Taxes (Income)	
Taxes (Real Estate)	
Home Mortgage (or Rent)	
Utilities (Electric, Gas, Water, sewer, cable)	
Maintenance	
Insurance (car)	
Food and Clothing	
Other Expenses (gas for cars)	
Tithing	
Credit Card #1	
Car Loan #1	
student Loan #1	
personal Loan #1	
Baby sitting	

I believe that knowing your expenses is one of the most important steps in the process of achieving financial freedom. When we know where our money is going, we can make smart decisions to manage and control them. The list of our expenses will help us clearly see all the debts we have logically and how we are making everybody rich while we are becoming poorer day by day. It is time to take our freedom seriously and get out of debts for life.

Luxury Expenses

Luxury expenses are expenses that are nice to have in life. They are not a necessity but they provide entertainment and enjoyment. They can keep us poor if we do not understand how to enjoy them without owning them. The strategy is to get our freedom first, then buy assets to pay for your luxury expenses. It is good to pay attention and use delayed gratification to advance our financial freedom as our priority. Then we can start accumulating luxury items as hobbies that can be worth more tomorrow like gold. Silver, antique cars, etc.

Here is an example of a luxury expenses list. Remember, you can always add to the list for your specific case.

LUXURY EXPENSES	
EXPENSE NAME	AMOUNT
Boats	
Designer bags	
Lots of toys for kids	
Cars	
Expensive watches	
Expensive vacations	

We get this example of expenses table by adding all three types of expenses together. Take a moment to update all your expenses as you continue to read. This is a practical book to help you master your money.

LIST OF ALL EXPENSES					
TAXES		**LIVING EXPENSES**		**LUXURY EXPENSES**	
NAME	**AMNT**	**EXPENSE NAME**	**AMNT**	**EXPENSE NAME**	**AMNT**
FED		Taxes (Income)			
STATE		Taxes (Real Estate)		Boat	
Medicare		Home Mortgage (or Rent)		Designer bags	
Medicaid		Utilities (Electric, Gas, Water, sewer, cable)		Lots of toys for kids	
Property		Maintenance		Cars	
Car		Insurance (car)		Expensive watches	
		Food and Clothing		Expensive vacations	
		Other Expenses (gas for cars)			
		Tithing			
		Credit Card #1			
		Car Loan #1			
		Student Loan #1			
		Personal Loan #1			
		Baby sitting			
		Phones			

Take some time to list all your expenses, as you are going to need them to use later in the chapters but, more importantly, to know where your money is going.

Principles learned that you need to practice

* *Expense is all money going out of your pocket or bank account. It is all money paid out for anything.*

* *A part of all income that you earn is yours to keep. At least 10% of each paycheck should be invested for your old age.*

* *The secret to financial freedom is to make, produce, or have more income than expenses.*

* *Expense is the financial concept that keeps people in the rate race of a job and poor.*

* *There are three main categories of expenses: Taxes, Living, and Luxuries.*

As we learn to control our expenses, we must also learn which expenses you need to get rid of. You just learned the toughest financial concept to master because it requires discipline, dedication, and planning. We now can proceed to the next chapter to learn what you can afford.

Chapter 6

NET INCOME OR CASH FLOW
(What you can really afford)

Financial term or concept 4: Our Net Income or Cash Flow

"Never take your eyes off the cash flow because it's the life blood of your financial life and your business." - Richard Branson

Like Branson said, cash flow is the life blood of a business, and it is also the life blood of your financial life. You will be able to build wealth for yourself as long as you start paying yourself first and have cash left after all expenses are paid every day or every month. Throughout my practice, I have learned that saving is not money to spend later. Instead, it is money to invest to increase your wealth and net worth. We will see how to do that when we get to section 3 of the book. I used to think like 90% to 95% of people in the United States; that, after retirement, my 401k would still be there for me. After 2008, most workers lost 40% to 60% of the money in their retirement accounts. I lost most of what I had in my 401k as well. I did not have an emergency fund, and I wasn't prepared to go two weeks without a paycheck on hand since I was living paycheck by paycheck. When the crisis hit, I was devastated; I needed a wake-up call to help me manage my money and take control of my financial life. I woke up in 2008 with a mission to financial independence. This book has been in the works for 12 years; you shouldn't wait until a crisis hits to decide to take care of your financial situation. You should decide today to manage your money and take control of your life. I believe, if you continue to apply these financial concepts and principles, you will always be prepared for any situation. I have been ready for any crisis since 2010, and I do not care if a democrat or a republican is in power. To me, it does not make a difference financially. I am also ready for any business or economic cycle. You can start this journey as well by implementing and following these financial principles in this book. I believe that in applying these principles in every area of your life, you will never be the same again. Let us look at net income and cash flow.

What is net income or cash flow?

Cash flow or net income is what is left after all the expenses have been paid. The cash flow determines your financial position. It tells you if you are cash poor or cash rich. Here is the income statement equation:

Income - Expenses = Net Income or Cash Flow

NET INCOME OR CASH FLOW	
	AMOUNT
Total Income	
Total Expenses	
INCOME - EXPENSES	
NET CASH FLOW	

If you have a negative cash flow, you are cash poor. If you have a negative cash flow, you have more expenses than income, meaning that you have to borrow money or use credit cards in order to pay expenses. If that is the case, you are bankrupt. You are living paycheck by paycheck. If you have a positive cash flow, you are cash rich. When you are cash flow positive, you can use the extra cash as capital to invest in assets to produce more cash. Then you are on your way to financial freedom.

Cash flow or net income is the key indicator for lenders. It provides to the bank or lender our cash position and our financial obligations. The lender uses our cash flow or net income to see how much we will be able to afford or pay back monthly. Pay close attention to your net cash flow or net income. At the end of each month, you can operate on a loss (- cash flow) or on a profit (+ cash flow).

Now it is time for you to put together your complete income statement. We will also look at 3 examples of income statements for your own practices.

Example of Income Statement

INCOME		
Earned Income		**Amount**
	Earned #1	
	Earned #2	
	Earned Total	
Passive Income		
	Real Estate	
	Business	
	Passive Total	
Portfolio Income		
	Interest	
	Dividends	
	Royalties	
	Portfolio Total	
TOTAL MONTHLY INCOME		

EXPENSES

TAXES		LIVING EXPENSES		LUXURY EXPENSES	
NAME	**AMNT**	**EXPENSE NAME**	**AMNT**	**EXPENSE NAME**	**AMNT**
FED		Taxes (Income)			
STATE		Taxes (Real Estate)		Boat	
Medicare		Home Mortgage (or Rent)		Designer bags	
Medicaid		Utilities (Electric, Gas, Water, sewer, cable)		Lots of toys for kids	
Property		Maintenance		Cars	
Car		Insurance (car)		Expensive watches	
		Food and Clothing		Expensive vacations	
		Other Expenses (gas for cars)			
		Tithing			
		Credit Card #1			
		Car Loan #1			
		Student Loan #1			
		Personal Loan #1			
		Baby sitting			
		Phones			

NET INCOME OR CASH FLOW	
	AMOUNT
Total Income	
Total Expenses	
INCOME - EXPENSES	
NET CASH FLOW	

Use this detailed model of an income statement to create your own income statement. Feel free to add to any item to reflect your specific situation.

For practical purposes, see the following three examples of personal statements for 3 different people.

Example 1: Self-employed Automotive technician ABC

INCOME		
Earned Income		**Amount**
	Earned #1	$ 4,500
	Earned #2	
	Earned Total	**$ 4,500**
Passive Income		
	Real Estate (NET)	$ 500
	Business	
	Passive Total	**$ 500**
Portfolio Income		
	Interest	
	Dividends	
	Royalties	
	Portfolio Total	
TOTAL MONTHLY INCOME		**$ 5,000**

EXPENSES					
TAXES		**LIVING EXPENSES**		**LUXURY EXPENSES**	
NAME	**AMNT**	**EXPENSE NAME**	**AMNT**	**EXPENSE NAME**	**AMNT**
FED	$ 250	Taxes (Income)			
STATE	$ 200	Taxes (Real Estate)		Boat	
Medicare	$ 160	Home Mortgage (or Rent)	$ 1300	Designer bags	
Medicaid	$140	Utilities (Electric, Gas, Water, sewer, cable)	$ 700	Lots of toys for kids	
Property		Maintenance	$ 100	Cars	
Car	$ 150	Insurance (car)	$ 155	Expensive watches	
		Food and Clothing	$ 150	Expensive vacations	
		Other Expenses (gas for cars)	$ 100		
		Tithing/donation	$ 400		
		Credit Card #1	$ 75		
		Car Loan #1			
		Student Loan #1			
		Personal Loan #1			
		Baby sitting			
		Phones	$120		
TOTAL	**$ 900**		**$ 3100**		**$ 0**

NET INCOME OR CASH FLOW	
	AMOUNT
Total Income	$ 5000
Total Expenses	$ 4000
INCOME - EXPENSES	
NET CASH FLOW	$ 1000

In this example, the technician is cash rich. The amount of money he or she spends is less than what he or she brings home. He or she has a cash flow of $1,000.00 a month. Looking at his or her income, he or she is already investing in real estate. With a net income of $1,000.00, he or she can continue to save for more real estate investment. He or she can also open an IRA (individual retirement account) to invest for his or her retirement. He or she is on his or her way to financial independence if he or she continues on this path.

Example 2: Health care worker Income Statement

INCOME		
Earned Income		**Amount**
	Earned #1	$ 10,500
	Earned #2	
	Earned Total	**$ 10,500**
Passive Income		
	Real Estate (NET)	
	Business	
	Passive Total	
Portfolio Income		
	Interest	
	Dividends	
	Royalties	
	Portfolio Total	
TOTAL MONTHLY INCOME		**$ 10,500**

EXPENSES					
TAXES		LIVING EXPENSES		LUXURY EXPENSES	
NAME	AMNT	EXPENSE NAME	AMNT	EXPENSE NAME	AMNT
FED	$ 400	Taxes (car)	$ 800		
STATE	$ 300	Taxes (Real Estate)	$ 600	Boat	$ 450
Medicare	$ 300	Home Mortgage (insurance)	$ 2400	Designer bags	
Medicaid	$ 280	Utilities (Electric, Gas, Water, sewer, cable)	$ 1200	Lots of toys for kids	
Property		Maintenance	$ 150	Cars	
401K	$ 720	Insurance (car)	$ 450	Expensive watches	
		Food and Clothing	$ 300	Expensive vacations	$ 300
		Other Expenses (gas for cars)	$ 150	Credit card 2	$ 350
		Tithing/ donation	$ 500		
		Credit Card #1	$ 250		
		Car Loan #1	$ 400		
		Student Loan #1	$700		
		Personal Loan #1			
		Baby sitting			
		Phones	$150		
TOTAL	$ 2000		$ 8100		$ 1100

NET INCOME OR CASH FLOW	
	AMOUNT
Total Income	$ 10,500
Total Expenses	$ 11,200
INCOME - EXPENSES	
NET CASH FLOW	$ (700)

It does not matter how much your income is; it all depends on how much you spend, how much you save, and how much you pay yourself. This health care professional is cash poor even though he or she makes a lot of money. He or she still is living paycheck by paycheck, much like 95% of people in the United States of America. Every month, he or she overspends by $700.00. He or she must either borrow money or work more overtime to bring in more income to cover all these expenses. If he or she gets rid of the luxury expenses and controls the other living expenses, he or she might be able to pay off his or her debt quicker or save money to buy assets for his or her long term financial independence.

Example 3: Engineer XYZ

INCOME		
Earned Income		**Amount**
	Earned #1	$ 6,000
	Earned #2	
	Earned Total	**$ 6,000**
Passive Income		
	Real Estate (NET)	$ 1,200
	Business (NET)	$ 5,000
	Passive Total	**$ 6,200**
Portfolio Income		
	Interest	
	Dividends	$ 75
	Royalties	
	Portfolio Total	**$ 75**
TOTAL MONTHLY INCOME		**$ 12,275**

EXPENSES

TAXES		LIVING EXPENSES		LUXURY EXPENSES	
NAME	**AMNT**	**EXPENSE NAME**	**AMNT**	**EXPENSE NAME**	**AMNT**
FED	$ 400	Taxes (car)	$ 600		
STATE	$ 250	Taxes (Real Estate)	$ 600	Boat	
Medicare	$ 250	Home Mortgage (insurance)	$1,200	Designer bags	
Medicaid	$ 240	Utilities (Electric, Gas, Water, sewer, cable)	$1,200	Lots of toys for kids	
		Maintenance	$ 150	Cars	
401K	$ 500	Insurance (car)	$ 300	Expensive watches	
		Food and Clothing	$ 300	Expensive vacations	$ 300
		Other Expenses (gas for cars)	$150	Credit card 2	$ 350
		Tithing/ Donation	$ 600		
		Credit Card #1	$ 200		
		Car Loan #1	$ 400		
		Student Loan #1	$ 600		
		Personal Loan #1			
		Baby sitting			
		Phones	$150		
Total Taxes	**$1,640**	**TOTAL LIVING EXPENSES**	**$ 6,450**	**TOTAL LUXURY EXP.**	**$ 650**
TOTAL EXPENSES			**$ 8,740.00**		

NET INCOME OR CASH FLOW	
	AMOUNT
Total Income	$ 12,275.00
Total Expenses	$ 8,740.00
INCOME - EXPENSES	
NET CASH FLOW	$ 3,535.00

This engineer manages his money well. He or she is close to achieving financial independence, but he or she needs to continue his or her financial education and increase his or her investment. A quick look at his or her financial statement reveals his or her secret: he or she has many streams of income, which takes discipline, delayed gratification, and risks to do what he or she is doing. He or she keeps expenses low, which increases his or her income and, in turn, increases net cash flow. Maybe we can take some strategies from this engineer on how to change our financial situation.

Principles learned that you need to practice

*   *Cash flow or net income is whatis left after all the expenses have been paid. The cash flow determines your cash position.*

*   *Saving is not money to spend later. It is money to invest to increase your wealth and your net worth.*

*   *If you have a negative cash flow, you have more expenses than income.*

*   *If you have a positive cash flow, you have more income than expenses.*

*   *The lender uses our cash flow or net income to see how much we will be able to afford or pay back monthly.*

You must become familiar with this concept and learn to apply it in order to find out what you can afford before you even apply for any loans. When you educate yourself, lenders might give you a change by lending you more money because you are financially responsible. In part 3 of the book, we will focus on financial position.

Part Three:

Financial position
(What are you worth)

Chapter 7

Balance sheet
(Financial Position)

Financial term or concept 5: Balance sheet or financial position

"Never invest in a company without understanding its finances. The biggest losses in stocks come from companies with poor balance sheets." - Peter Lynch

Now that you know your cash position, it is time really to change your finances for good. If your cash position is negative, you must start controlling your expenses to spend less than your income so you need to do that in order to start building cash deposits to start buying assets. If you have positive cash flow and savings, you are ready to take advantage of your cash position to start building your assets for your long-term financial freedom. When I learned about balance sheets, assets, liabilities, and net worth, I realized that financial freedom is right around the corner. I could do this as long as I am disciplined, take control of my expenses, and start to invest in assets.

I have to give credit to Robert Kiyosaki for his 2 books that I keep reading today: "Rich Dad, Poor Dad" and "Cash Flow Quadrant." Robert took the time to explain how important assets are as a source of cash. He also explains how to turn liabilities into assets. He believes that everyone should take care of his or her own financial life. I was convinced by reading his books that I must do this if I want to retire the way I want. I needed to do this for my legacy, my kids, and my family. Robert helped me get over my fear of beginning this journey and acquiring assets for my financial freedom. My book will teach you how to apply these financial concepts to your financial life with concrete examples that you can follow to remove your fear. I would advise anyone who is serious about financial freedom to read those 2 books if you have not done so.

I will keep these chapters short so you can spend more time practicing these concepts in your life. Do not forget to apply and implement the financial principles; they will make the difference in your life, not the knowing only. 7 years ago, I was in training, learning how to buy real estate for passive income when I started learning about assets, liabilities, and net worth. The rich have known these principles since the Babylonian Empire. Even before the invention of money and the banking system, kings and landowners have been using these principles to gain an advantage on regular people and workers, while the poor have never had a chance to learn these principles in school. Why don't we learn about money and finance in school since money is the life blood of wealth and the financial system of this world? My purpose for the rest of my life is to turn everyone into a successful entrepreneur, investor, and business owner. After reading this book, you shouldn't have an excuse for not being wealthy and successful. This is the time to start learning about the money-producing financial concepts. Let us begin with a balance sheet.

What is the Balance Sheet?
According to Finish Rich Dictionary by Davis Bach, the balance sheet is the statement of the assets, liabilities, and capital of a business or other organization at a point in time.

Balance sheet is the statement of assets and liabilities of a business or institution, according to the American Heritage Dictionary.

The balance sheet is a record of all we own, all we owe,

and what we are worth at any point in time (weekly, monthly, quarterly, yearly). The balance sheet tells bankers, lenders, and others our net worth or financial position. We need to become familiar with our balance sheet and pay close attention to it. Like the cash flow, net worth is a key indicator for lenders and cost of borrowing money. If we need to borrow money to invest or consume, the lender will need to see our income statement as well as our balance sheet. It is important to know it because the balance sheet will tell them exactly what they can get if we default on the loan. In other words, the balance sheet tells lenders what assets you own that can be used as collateral.

The balance sheet has 3 main components: assets, liabilities, and net worth for a person or owner's equity for businesses. Let us look at a detailed balance sheet before we go to each one separately.

ASSETS		
LIQUID	Bank Accounts (cash)	
	Stocks	
	Deposits	
PHYSICAL (tangible)	Real Estate (NET) 1	
	Real Estate (NET) 2	
	Business Value (NET)	
INTANGIBLE	Intellectual property	
	Patent / Royalty	
	401k	
ASSETS TOTAL		

LIABILITIES		
GOOD DEBTS	Credit Card 1	
	Car Loans	
	School Loans	
	Home Mortgage	
	Other Debt (real estate rental 1)	
	Other Debt (real estate rental 2)	
BAD DEBTS	Personal Loans 2	
	Boat loan	
	Credit card 2	
	Car Loans 2	
TOTAL LIABILITIES		

NET WORTH or EQUITY
ASSET = LIABILITIES + EQUITY
NET WORTH or EQUITY = ASSETS - LIABILITIES

Before you learn about assets, liabilities, and net worth in the following chapters, take some time to see if you can fill out your balance sheet. You should update the balance sheet every month, quarter, or year. You should be ready at any time because opportunities will come to you to buy assets once you start buying assets for income. People will start bringing you money to invest for them like you would not believe. Banks will start calling you and sending you emails about all the loans that they can give you to continue your investments and businesses.

Principles learned that you need to practice

* *The balance sheet is a record of all we own, all*

we owe, and what we are worth at any point in time (weekly, monthly, quarterly, yearly)

* *The balance sheet has 3 main components: assets, liabilities, and net worth for a person or owner's equity for businesses.*

This section of the book is one of the most important sections for you to practice because you will start learning how to buy things that can make you money. You will start learning that you do not have to decrease your standard of living or expenses, but you must buy assets to pay for your expenses. Keep reading and practice.

Chapter 8

Assets
(How to produce money)

Financial term or concept 6: Asset

"Assets put money in your pocket, whether you work or not, and liabilities take money from your pocket." - Robert Kiyosaki

One of the most important financial concepts that I learned to apply in my financial life is assets. The more assets you acquire, the more wealth you will own. Assets are like trees because they produce fruits at specific times, repeatedly. When I learned that assets could repeatedly produce money or income at certain times, like monthly (passive income) until you sell it, I realized being rich is not about paper money at all. Being rich is all about applying financial principles that you are learning in this book. I understand why the Bible says that people are dying for lack of knowledge. Once I knew that assets could set me free from the slavery of a job, I was free instantly. But I did not realize it was going to take me discipline, delayed gratification, and planning. It took a lot of time to go from a mindset of poverty to an mindset of abundance. That is why I started the book with mindset, discipline, and planning. You have the challenge of changing your mindset to start your financial freedom journey. Asset is more than a word; it is a way of thinking, and a lifestyle to apply in every opportunity that we have. I believe that, before you spend money on anything, you need to know which one of your assets will be paying for it. If you do not have an asset to pay for an expense, you should borrow the money in order to buy this asset. The asset, then, will pay for the expense. You should get into debt only if you are buying assets that will pay for itself and put more money in your pocket. Let us look at assets.

What is an asset?
According to the American Heritage Dictionary, assets are all properties, such as stocks or cash that may cover the liabilities of a person or business.

Assets are property owned by a person or company regarded as having value and available to meet debts, commitment, or legacies, according to the Finish Rich dictionary by David Bach.

I conclude that assets are everything of value someone, or a company, owns,. Value is anything that we own that can produce income or provide us money. Assets can make us rich and increase our wealth. We can pass on our assets to our kids, and they can pass them on to their kids, and so on for generations. Our financial goal should be to acquire as many assets we can, until they can pay for all our expenses in life. Assets are producers of values. Anything that can give value to people can turn into assets. If we look at our life, what are the things we value? Why do we value one thing over another? What do people value? Can we find a way to give people what they value instead of what we value? As I was selling shoes in the flea market in Laurel, Delaware, I discovered that people would pay more money for what they value. I remember one kid who wanted colorful Nike Air Force Ones, but the price was $70 because they were popular and rare. The problem was, his mother did not want to buy it because of the price. He valued the pair of shoes so much that his mother had to come back the next day to buy them for him. The shoes were an asset for me because they were valuable to the young man. As we continue to turn ideas and things into assets, we need to learn how to produce value to others.

There are many types of assets or asset classes. We will

cover liquid assets, physical assets, and intangible assets. Feel free to fill out all your assets as you are reading. This book is designed for you to practice your financial skills as you go through it.

ASSETS		
LIQUID	Bank Accounts (cash)	
	Stocks	
	Deposits	
PHYSICAL	Real Estate (NET) 1	
	Real Estate (NET) 2	
	Business Value (NET)	
INTANGIBLE	Intellectual property	
	Patent / Royalty	
	401k	
ASSETS TOTAL		

Liquid Assets

Liquid assets are assets that can be converted into cash quickly and easily. Examples of liquid assets are cash, stocks, and deposits.

Liquid Asset example 1: Cash

Think about cash in terms of value: why is cash so valuable? Cash is so valuable because we need it for every financial transaction under the sun. A means of exchange has been the sole priority of men since the beginning of time. The invention of paper money has made development possible. Money is just a derivative of value. You do not create money without value. Every product, thing, and service can produce and bring money as a means of exchange. Cash is just a reward for exchanging value. Liquid assets are nothing but the quick exchange of value from one person to the other. Cash is an asset because it gives you the ability to acquire things that can produce more cash. That is why people say, "you need money to make money." All they are saying is that, once you have cash, it is easier to make more of it because you will be able to take advantage of more opportunities. The cash in your pocket can open the door to a different life for you if you learn and practice these financial principles. I always say that practice makes improvement and development.

Liquid Asset example 2: Stocks

What is a stock?
A stock is a partial owning of a company or an enterprise. It is a share or a piece of a company. A stock owner has a claim on future earnings or profits of a company. The stock owner is part owner of the company or enterprise.

What makes a stock valuable?
A stock is valuable because it is a derivative of a company that provides value to people and society. Again, a derivative is part of something bigger or derived from something else. The stock's value is based on the company's value. The more valuable the company, the more valuable the stock, and the higher the price of the stock. These financial concepts are so valuable for us to learn because they help us analyze companies as well. The great investor of our time, Warren Buffett, says

"When you buy a stock, you buy the company, and we should never invest in what we do not understand."

He is right, and we should learn what makes a company valuable to us. The value of the company is determined by the value of the service and products that are offered to its customers. By looking at the company balance sheet and income statement, we can see the value reflected in the sales, income, net income, liabilities, and assets of companies. We need to earn stock as part of our portfolio of passive income.

What makes stock valuable to us as investors?

Stock, as assets, is valuable to us in two ways. First, stock appreciates in value as the company increases in value. For example, if you buy the Apple stock for $5 back when, your stock would appreciate to $110 or more today, which is over 220% increased in value. Secondly, some stocks pay a dividend. Dividend is a sharing of the profit of the company. Workers of companies including CEOs and executives are working for the owners who are the shareholders or stockholders. Every 3 months, the company is paying the owners in dividend as part of the equity and net income. I would rather be the owner of a company than an employee, and so would most others. If the company is not doing well, the employees will be fired, but the owners cannot be fired. I want to be an owner from now on.

Physical or tangible Assets

Physical assets are assets that can be touched, felt, and seen. They cannot be converted into cash quickly and easily. Examples of physical assets are real estate, businesses, and trademarks. Tangible assets, like any other asset, produce income. Tangible assets only mean we can touch and see the physical presence, which gives some people peace of mind.

Let us take an example of real estate as a tangible asset.

We are not talking about your house that you have a mortgage on. If you have a mortgage and you are paying every month, you do not really own the house. The bank owns your house. You are working for the bank or lenders. Even after you pay off your mortgage, you still need to pay your taxes as liabilities, says Robert

Kiyosaki. If you do not pay your taxes, the city or state can take your house. The house is turned into an asset when you use it to make money. You need to know that clearly because the bankers will not teach about these financial principles. When you buy a multifamily to rent to people, they are paying you every month. Then, you can say you have an asset if your monthly cost is lower than the income received. You need to learn these principles for your own financial freedom.

Intangible Assets

Intangible assets are assets that do not have a physical existence. They cannot be seen or touched. Examples of intangible assets are Intellectual property, permits, royalties, 401k…

Intangible assets are like any other assets because they produce income. Intangible assets do not have a physical presence, but they are powerful assets. Much like an invisible force in the minds of people. People and organizations can read your book and use your patent for a fee, which is income to you. Your purpose in life, if you accept it, is to produce something, distribute it, and sell it to as many people as possible for as long as possible. This is asset creation at its finest. We need to learn these principles for our real freedom.

When it comes to assets, our goal should be to accumulate as many as possible until they can produce enough income to cover all our expenses and liabilities. That is financial freedom.

Principles learned that you need to practice
  * *Assets are everything of value someone owns, or a company owns.*

  * *Assets are producers of value. Anything that can give value to people can turn into assets.*

  * *Financial freedom is when your assets can*

produce enough income to cover all your expenses and more.

*

*   *There are many types of assets or asset classes: liquid assets, physical assets, and intangible assets*

Use the asset template to list all your assets. If you do not have any assets, it is your time to practice this important financial concept you just learned to start creating and accumulating assets. Now you understand and see how important assets are; let us move to liabilities that are stealing your money in broad daylight.

Chapter 9

Liabilities
(What takes money from you)

Financial term or concept 7: Liability

"Liabilities are just assets in hiding." - Mark Victor Hansen

Liabilities are the things that take money away from us. Liabilities can change to assets, like Mark Hansen says. I can remember when I was proud of buying a Mercedes-Benz on credit. I was saying that the Benz is my greatest asset. Now I realize that I was misled financially. I was buying all the shining things that were losing value daily. Before we buy stuff, we need to know how to turn the stuff into assets if we want to. I would advise you not to attach yourself to things that can be destroyed any time. However, you should plan to know how to build and create things. It is better to know how to create, transform, and build assets. While learning about debt and liabilities, it dawned on me that they are the new form of slavery. You are working to pay your new master of lenders and bankers until you are dead. You could never be free from a job if you are constantly in debt. Your debt keeps you slave in the rat race forever because your mortgage and your car loan are owned by your master. The Bible told us that the borrower is a slave to the lender. Why do we keep borrowing instead of lending? We need to learn to turn liability into assets in order to gain our freedom.

What is liability?

Liability is a thing for which someone is responsible for,

a debt or a financial obligation, according to David Bach in the Finish Rich dictionary.

Also, according to the American heritage dictionary, liability is something for which one is liable for: obligation, responsibility, or debt. It is something that holds one back, handicap.

When I look at how 95% of people around the world live, I now know why people are in poverty. Liability, like the American heritage dictionary says, holds people back. Debt and liabilities keep the 95% of the world population in poverty. It is our time to break the chain of poverty with financial wisdom.

After all my research and reading, I like the definition that says liability is anything that takes money out of your pocket or your bank account on a regular basis. It is what you owe that requires payment. Liability can be good or bad. We need to know what good liability is and what is bad liability.

Model of liabilities or debt

LIABILITIES		
GOOD DEBTS	Credit Card 1	
	Car Loans	
	School Loans	
	Home Mortgage	
	Other Debt (real estate rental 1)	
	Other Debt (real estate rental 2)	
	Business loan	
BAD DEBTS	Personal Loans 2	
	Boat loan	
	Credit card 2	
	Car Loans 2	
	Timeshare loan	
TOTAL LIABILITIES		

Take the time to fill out the model for your own liabilities. You can add to the list for your specific case.

Good liabilities

Good liabilities, or good debts, are debts that can make you money or increase your net worth. When we think about good debt, we should think about, "can it bring income or money?" or what can we do to turn it into money? Can someone else pay for it? It all depends on how you see and use debt that makes all the difference. We need to start training our mind to see possibilities that liabilities or debts can offer us. For some of us, it can take a major event to have this paradigm shift. It took me the financial crisis of 2008 to change my mindset and my behavior about money. We need to keep reminding ourselves that our financial system is based on debt. The more the federal reserve and the banks print money, the less our paper money is worth. A dollar today could be worth more than a dollar tomorrow because of inflation. Debt can help you if we study the money system, understand the system, and use the system correctly. Financial education is the key.

Bad Liabilities

Bad liabilities, or bad debts, are debts that take money from you or decrease your net worth. We must realize that the use is what makes a difference when we say a liability can be both good and bad. When it comes to bad debt or liability, we should think about how much it will cost. How long will we pay for it? Because we use debt to buy things, we should know all our options to keep costs down. We should keep debt as short term as possible. Debt or bad liability can keep you in slavery for the rest of your life. Debt can keep you in depression, and some people have nervous breakdowns because of it. Freedom is a mental state. Money can have a major impact on our mental health and physical life. You should take the full advantage of this book to practice money management and earn your freedom. How do you know that you have a bad debt? When the thing that you acquire is losing value daily, you know it is a liability. You will also know when you must go to work to pay for it month after month. Here a list of things that can be liability if you buy them on credit: cars, furniture, appliances, clothes, shoes etc.

Let us look at a couple of examples:

1) Home mortgage

    Good liability: If we buy a house at a low price, we did some work to increase the value. Or, if we buy the property, we rent it for monthly cash flow.

    Bad liability: If we just buy a house at a high price, we live in it and we are making monthly payments ourselves. We do not have any room for appreciation.

2) Credit cards

    Good debts: We can use the credit on your card to put a down payment on rental property. The property is paying back the balance with the interest every month. Also, we can use our credit card to get cash back on purchase and pay the balance as quickly as possible and on time. We can use the credit to buy a car to use for uber or taxi.

    Bad debts: We use our credit card to buy clothes or go to vacation. We pay the minimum payment every month. My furniture is on credit cards and makes lower payment for 5 to 10 years.

Principles learned that you need to practice
* *Liability is anything that takes money out of your pocket or your bank account on a regular basis.*

* *Liability can be good or bad, and it all depends on how you use it.*

* *Good liabilities, or good debts, are debts that can make you money or increase your net worth.*

* *Bad liabilities, or bad debts, are debts that take money from you or decrease your net worth.*

Now that we know what liabilities are and how to use them, let us learn net worth in the next chapter.

Chapter 10

Net Worth or Net Value or Equity (What you really own)

Financial term or concept 8: Net worth or net value or equity

"Time and health are two precious assets that we don't recognize and appreciate until they have been depleted." - Denis Waitley

We must pay close attention to our financial wealth and how we spend our time in life. Our financial worth will determine how we spend our time. We should not take our financial life lightly. Money is extremely important in life under the sun. Money determines where we live. Money determines the quality of care that we will receive. Money determines what schools our kids go to. Money determines the impact we make in this life. Money helps us achieve our purpose in life. Money determines how we can affect next generations. Money is power. That is why people are killing for it. We need to understand it and how to create it. We should not take the significance of our financial position lightly. Let us look at net worth.

What is net worth or financial equity?

According to the American Heritage dictionary, the net worth is what remains after all deductions or adjustments have been made.

Net worth or net value is what is left as economic value after all liabilities have been paid from all the assets. here is what the equations look like:

NET WORTH or EQUITY	
ASSET = LIABILITIES + EQUITY	
NET WORTH or EQUITY = ASSETS - LIABILITIES	

Net worth or equity might be positive or negative, like net income. We are running in a surplus as long as the net worth is positive. That also means that we have more assets than liabilities. When the net worth is negative, we are running a deficit. We are bankrupt. That also means that we have more liabilities or debt than assets.

Let us bring the balance sheet together for the 3 examples that we had in the income statement chapter.

Example 1: Balance sheet of the Self-employed Automotive technician ABC

ASSETS		
LIQUID	Bank Accounts (cash)	$5,000.00
	Stocks	$15,000.00
	Deposits	
PHYSICAL	Real Estate (NET) 1	$200,000.00
	Real Estate (NET) 2	
	Business Value (NET)	
INTANGIBLE	Intellectual property	
	Patent / Royalty	
	401k	$50,000.00
ASSETS TOTAL		**$270,000.00**

LIABILITIES		
GOOD DEBTS	Credit Card 1	$1,000.00
	Car Loans	
	School Loans	
	Home Mortgage	$150,000.00
	Other Debt (real estate rental 1)	$110,000.00
	Other Debt (real estate rental 2)	
	Business loan	
BAD DEBTS	Personal Loans 2	
	Boat loan	
	Credit card 2	
	Car Loans 2	
	Timeshare loan	
TOTAL LIABILITIES		**$ 261,000.00**

NET WORTH or EQUITY	
ASSET = LIABILITIES + EQUITY	
NET WORTH or EQUITY = ASSETS - LIABILITIES	**$9,000.00**

By reviewing the balance sheet of the technician, you can see that he or she is worth $9,000.00. If he or she has to liquidate all the assets to pay all the liabilities or debts, he or she will worth $9k. We will see how important the net worth is in the next chapter when we talk about buying power. He or she can increase his or her net worth by buying more assets while keeping the liabilities the same. The technician is in a good financial position. He or she can borrow more money to increase his or her financial position even more.

Example 2: Health care worker balance sheet

ASSETS		
LIQUID	Bank Accounts (cash)	$10,000.
	Stocks	
	Deposits	
PHYSICAL	Real Estate (NET) 1	
	Real Estate (NET) 2	
	Business Value (NET)	
INTANGIBLE	Intellectual property	
	Patent / Royalty	
	401k	$150,000
ASSETS TOTAL		**$160,000**

LIABILITIES		
GOOD DEBTS	Credit Card 1	$3,000
	Car Loans	$45,000
	School Loans	$60,000
	Home Mortgage	$400,000
	Other Debt (real estate rental 1)	
	Other Debt (real estate rental 2)	
	Business loan	
BAD DEBTS	Personal Loans 2	
	Boat loan	$20,000
	Credit card 2	$4,000
	Car Loans 2	
	Timeshare loan	$10,000
TOTAL LIABILITIES		**$542,000**

NET WORTH or EQUITY	
ASSET = LIABILITIES + EQUITY	
NET WORTH or EQUITY = ASSETS - LIABILITIES	**($382,000)**

The health care worker has a negative net worth. He or she is bankrupt. He or she has more liabilities or debts than assets, even though he or she has a higher monthly income. He or she is running a deficit of $362,000.00. In that case, he or she must increase the amount of work he or she puts in or borrow money in order to pay his or her liabilities. He or she needs to cut some of these liabilities and get out of debts if he or she wants to start on the road to financial independence, which is very possible with his or her high income. The health care worker is in a bad financial position. It would be hard to borrow more money from any lender.

Example 3: Balance sheet of Engineer XYZ

ASSETS		
LIQUID	Bank Accounts (cash)	$20,000
	Stocks	$10,000
	Deposits	
PHYSICAL	Real Estate (NET) 1	$ 375,000
	Real Estate (NET) 2	
	Business Value (NET)	$ 75,000
INTANGIBLE	Intellectual property	
	Patent / Royalty	
	401k	$125,000
ASSETS TOTAL		**$605,000**

LIABILITIES		
GOOD DEBTS	Credit Card 1	$1,500
	Car Loans	$25,000
	School Loans	$30,000
	Home Mortgage	$200,000
	Other Debt (real estate rental 1)	$85,000
	Other Debt (real estate rental 2)	$110,000
	Business loan	$25,000
BAD DEBTS	Personal Loans 2	
	Boat loan	
	Credit card 2	$500
	Car Loans 2	
	Timeshare loan	
TOTAL LIABILITIES		$476,500

NET WORTH or EQUITY		
ASSET = LIABILITIES + EQUITY		
NET WORTH or EQUITY = ASSETS - LIABILITIES		**$128,500**

The engineer has a positive net worth of $128,500.00. He or she is running a surplus. He or she has more assets than liabilities. With good credit, his or her buying power can take him or her to the next level financially quickly. He or she needs to continue buying more assets until they can cover both his or her expenses and liabilities.

Principles learned that need to practice

* *Net worth or net value is what is left as economic value after all liabilities have been paid from all the assets.*

* *When the net worth is positive, you are running a surplus.*

* *When the net worth is negative, you are running a deficit. You are bankrupt.*

Before continuing to section 4 of the book, let us look at the flow of money for 7 types of financial statements. We are going to apply everything- concept of position, cash flow, income statement, and financial statement or balance sheet to retirement. These examples will clarify how money flows from income statement to balance sheet. The same flow occurs in businesses and governments.

7 Examples of Flow of money between Financial Statements (Income statement + Balance Sheet)

1) Rate Race Financial Statement (employee)

Your Job

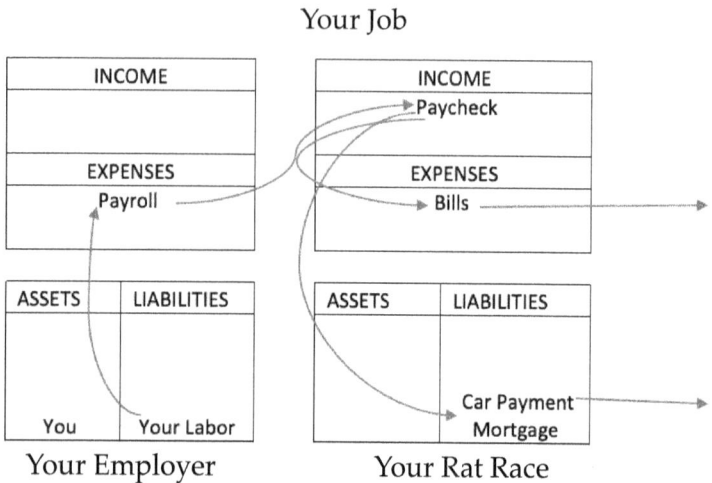

	INCOME
	EXPENSES
Payroll	

ASSETS	LIABILITIES
You	Your Labor

	INCOME
	Paycheck
	EXPENSES
	Bills

ASSETS	LIABILITIES
	Car Payment
	Mortgage

Your Employer   Your Rat Race

If you are an employee, you are in the rat race with a financial statement like this one. In this case, there are 2 financial statements: your employer and yourself. By looking at the employer statement, you are both an asset and a liability. You produce labor that is transformed into money, and, as an expense, the company must pay you. Every pay period, money flows from your employer payroll as a paycheck to you as income in your income statement. Now, the money game begins. In this case, the money then flows to all the expenses and all the debts (liabilities). At the end of the day, this person pays everyone else, and there is no money left to buy assets for emergencies. If you look at the asset column, it is blank. There is no cash or money producing asset. This person needs to continue working until they are dead in the rat race. This person does not realize that he or she is cash poor because he or she still has a job. By observing the flow of money, his or her money is going out to pay someone else. Take time to compare your financial statement to this employee's financial statement. If this person gets fired or sick, the flow of money to his or her income statement stops. This is a troubling position to be in, but 95% of the US population is in the scenario.

2) Pension retirement Financial Statement

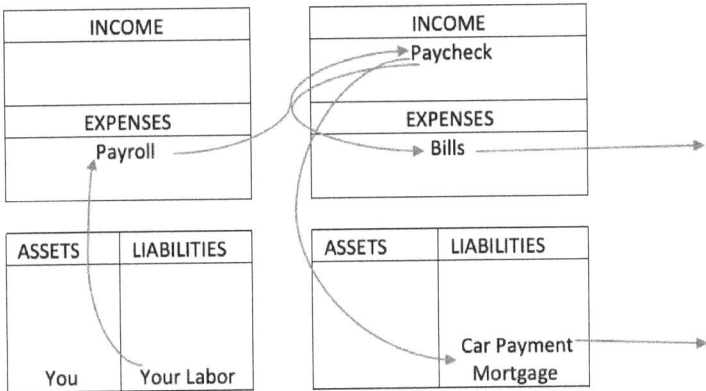

GOODBYE TENSION HELLO PENSION!

INCOME		INCOME	
		Paycheck	
EXPENSES		EXPENSES	
Payroll		Bills	

ASSETS	LIABILITIES	ASSETS	LIABILITIES
			Car Payment
You	Your Labor		Mortgage

Employer/Social Security   Your Rat Race

In the case of this person with a pension, he or she can relax a little bit in retirement as long as the company that he or she worked for his or her life does not go out of business or fill bankruptcy. He or she will receive a paycheck for the rest of his or her life. The baby boomers have this gift, but pensions no longer exist. This person also collects Medicare, and his or her house is paid for. Every month, money flows from his or her former employer pension, and Social Security to his or her income statement. From his or her income, money flows to expenses and the liabilities for the property. Even though the house does not have a mortgage on it, the tax and insurance must be paid. At least, at the end of the month, he or she has enough money left to enjoy life and retirement. If trouble comes his or her way, he or she can sell the house (the only asset he or she owns). Some financial experts like Robert Kiyosaki might not even consider the house as an asset because it is consuming cash in tax and insurance. The house is not producing cash flow.

3) Retirement with Medicare only

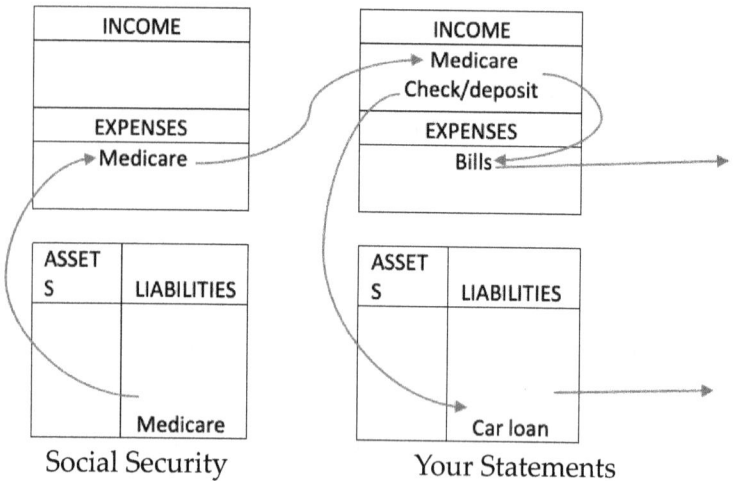

THIS IS OUR RETIREMENT PLAN.

INCOME		INCOME	
		Medicare Check/deposit	
EXPENSES		EXPENSES	
Medicare		Bills	

ASSETS	LIABILITIES	ASSETS	LIABILITIES
	Medicare		Car loan

Social Security   Your Statements

In case 3, this couple retired with the social security checks only. Every month, money flows from the government (Medicare) to the couple's income statement. Even though the couple does not have a mortgage, they still must pay rent as part of expenses and the car note as liability. Due to this, the couple may not have a need to beg or go back to work in order to earn additional income. This is hard to see since we are living in the best of times. This couple most likely did not have a financial education. We should not let this happen to us. The couple do not own any assets that they can rely on for income. This is a disaster when someone depends on the government totally for his or her income.

4) Retirement with 401k, saving, IRA Financial statement, and Medicare

"If you work hard and invest wisely, you can afford to turn 65 on your 80th birthday."

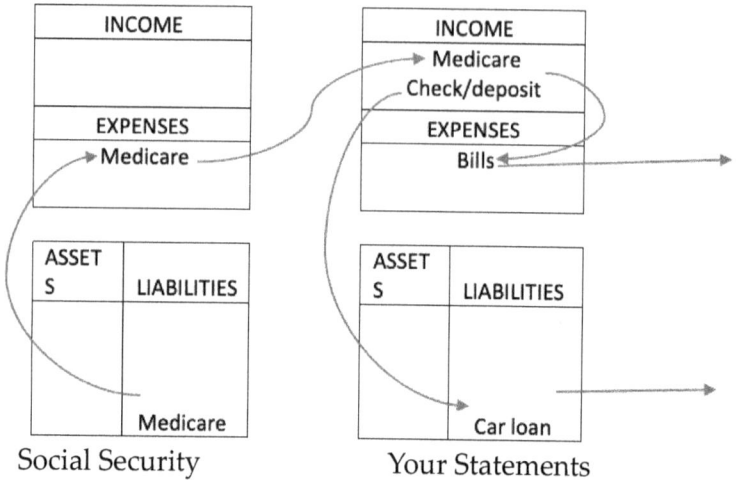

Social Security   Your Statements

In his case, money is coming from three sources. He has Medicare, 401k, and IRA (individual retirement account). He might have to downgrade his lifestyle, so his money can last for his long retirement since people are expected to live 15 to 20 years after retirement. He must keep his money invested and redraw a small amount of his 401k and IRA. He can run out of money very soon if he does not manage his money well. A lot of people run out of money well into retirement because they do not plan and continue to invest even though they are in retirement. They must go back to work to earn income to continue their lifestyle. Most people downsize to keep expenses low so they can enjoy retirement. He might have to sell his house to buy small condo cash with the equity, so he can get rid of the mortgage on his house. Or he can also sell the single family to buy a multifamily with 3 or 4 apartments. While the tenants are paying for the mortgage with potential additional cash flow, he can live in one apartment for free.

5) Bankruptcy financial statement

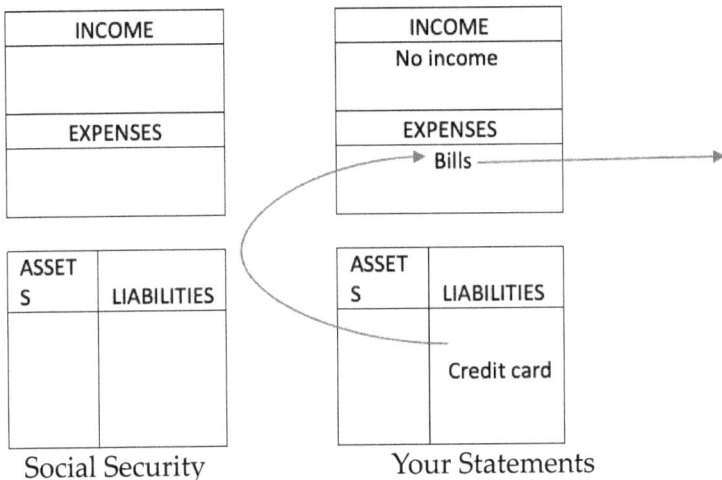

INCOME
EXPENSES

INCOME
No income
EXPENSES
Bills ———————▶

ASSETS	LIABILITIES

ASSETS	LIABILITIES
	Credit card

Social Security   Your Statements

In case 5, this person is bankrupt. He or she has no income. By now, we know that everyone has expenses, even babies. This individual must find a new way of income. When someone is bankrupt, he or she is borrowing money to pay for expenses. He or she cannot pay his or her liabilities because there is no income or not enough income. We need to avoid this situation at all costs. This person is using his or her credit card, which is a liability to pay for expenses. What is going to happen when the credit card reaches its limit? Trouble is at his or her door. He or she needs to find a job or move in with someone who can support him or her. It is a painful situation to be in.

6) Financial Freedom Financial statement

    A) Freedom while in the rat race

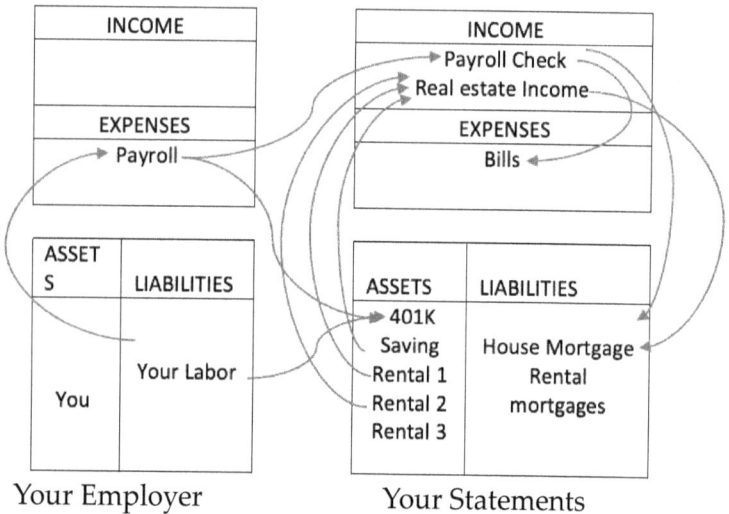

Your Employer   Your Statements

You can still achieve financial freedom while you are still working, like in case 6A. As you can see in this case, this person has multiple sources of income: his job and 3 income properties. He or she will be able to achieve financial freedom as long as he or she continues to acquire more income property. He or she will have the choice to continue to work because he or she loves his or her job. He or she also will continue to build his or her retirement account by increasing contribution or increasing his or her cash for emergencies. No matter what happens in the economy, he or she is ready for anything. This is the position that we all should be in financially. Can you put yourself in that position? You will be able to get there if you follow and implement the principles in this book. This person can work until 62 to retire with additional income from social security, and he or she can pay off the mortgage early. With no mortgage on his or her primary residence, retirement looks better and better. He or she can start building his or her legacy for future generations.

B) Freedom outside the rat race

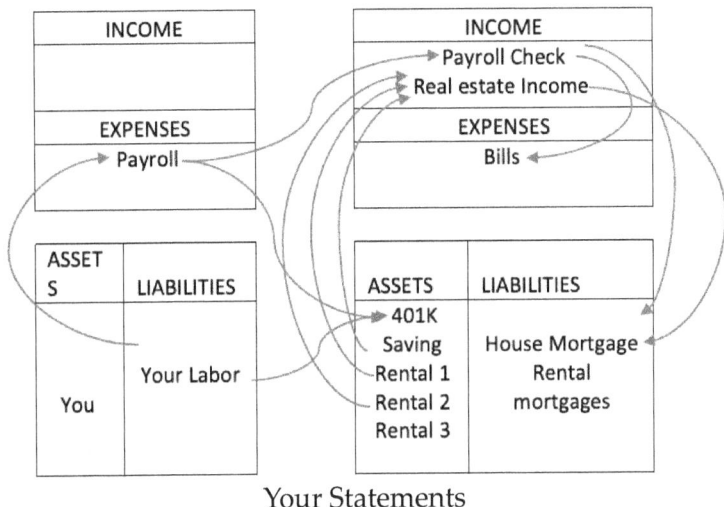

Your Statements

In case 6B, this individual creates and begins their own business and, on the side, invests in the stock market. The business can provide more income as it becomes successful, and the stocks can provide dividend every quarter. In this case, he or she is out of the rat race. He or she is financially independent. His or her assets can outlast his or her life. He or she can still pass the assets to future generations. In this case, he or she has options because he or she can continue to acquire real estate and hire people to run the business. He or she can hire management companies to run everything. He or she can enjoy life in his or her own terms. Life is beautiful. You also can achieve this financial position by applying the principles in this book.

7) Government financial statement

   A) Irresponsible Government, slave his people

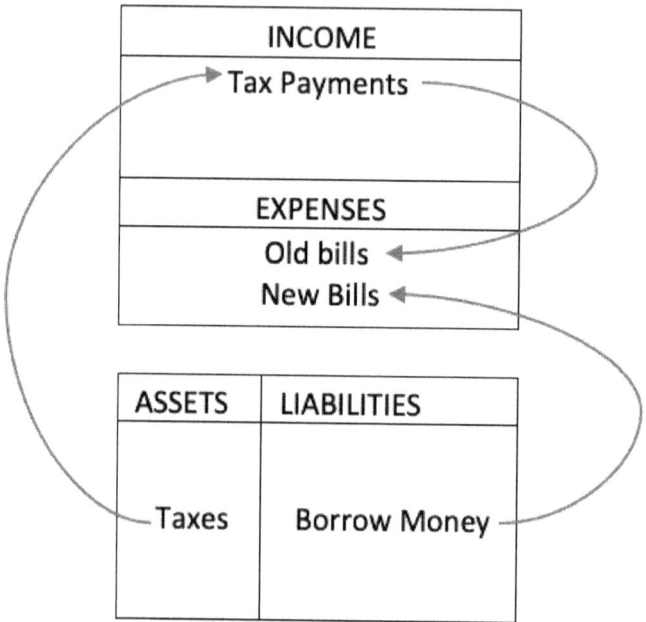

In case 7A, the government is irresponsible and big. They are involved in wars that they cannot pay for, and they create a lot of social programs. As we know, the government is the worst at creating jobs. They are better at spending tax money. Due to this, the government must borrow money or print more money if taxes are not enough to support government expenses. This government is bankrupt, but they have the advantage of the printing press. They can print as much money as they want. When the government prints money, your money is worth less in the marketplace. This process of printing money creates inflation. Big Government is taking future money from future generations to pay for expenses today. Future generations will have to pay more taxes and become slaves of the political system.

B) Responsible Government, Free his people

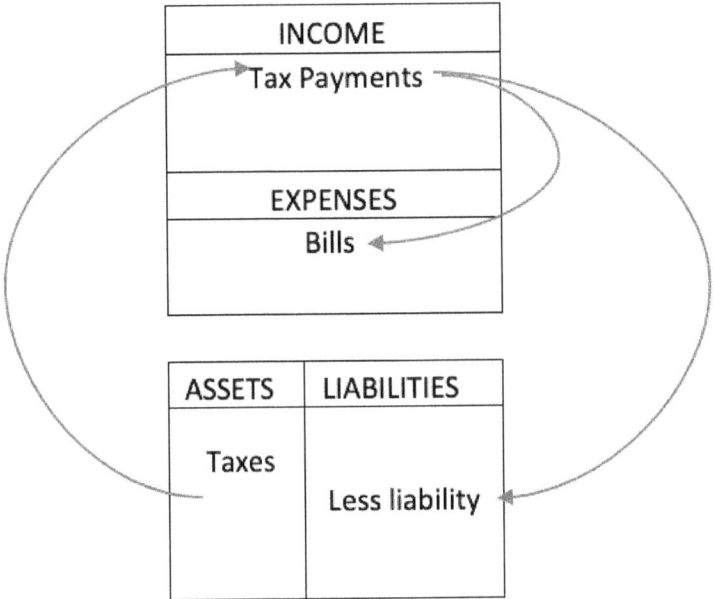

INCOME
Tax Payments
EXPENSES
Bills

ASSETS	LIABILITIES
Taxes	
	Less liability

In case 7B, the government is small and responsible. The government keeps spending under control. The income from taxes is enough to pay the expenses for the government. This is fiscal responsibility on the part of the political leaders. It also helps the government contribute to creating more jobs and promote entrepreneurs. Private enterprise and small business are the driving force of economic development and job creation. The job of the government in this case is to provide security, infrastructure, and good education. We need to get involved in the political system to keep the government small and pro-business.

Part Four:

Buying power
(What can you afford)

Chapter 11

Buying Power
(What others trust you with)

Financial term or concept 9: Buying Power

"In an economic capitalist system, consumer's buying power is the driving force of the economy."-Sezair Julien

The concept of buying power is based on your trust level, history, assets, liability, and income. School does not teach these principles that play a major role in our financial life. Therefore, I put this book together to coach you through these financial principles that everyone should apply every day. Again, not only should you get the knowledge from this book, you must apply them in order to make a difference in your financial life.

What is buying power?
Buying power is a compound word that consists of 2 powerful words: buy and power. Let us look each word separately on a financial perspective:

* **Buy or buying**

   Buying is to acquire in exchange for money, according to the American Heritage Dictionary. You can buy up, which is to purchase all that is available. You can also buy out, which is to purchase the entire holding of an owner. We can also buy back, which is the buying back of goods, stocks by the original seller, according to the Finish Rich Dictionary by David Bach.

* **Power**

>   Power is the ability or capacity to perform or act effectively. It also means to control or influence.

Buying power, then, is the capability and power of purchasing things like cars, clothes, and foods. It also gives us the ability and power to acquire assets like real estates, stocks, or businesses with cash or credit. Your buying power can derive from 4 sources, in my opinion.

1) Cash that you have on hands

>   Therefore, saving, not spending all the money we earn, staying out of debts, and increasing your income potential are all so important. From them, we receive the ability to control our financial life. We need to keep some cash as capital for unexpected opportunities in life. They will come, but the question is "Will we be ready?" How much cash do you have in reserve? If I present you with a financial opportunity, can you act now? This is buying power in action. Cash is king, like it says.

2) The assets that we own

>   Our net worth increases due to the value of the assets we own as long as we keep our liabilities under control. Our assets give us the ability to produce income. It also gives us the ability to liquidate or sell some of our holdings for cash in order to buy or participate in bigger and better opportunities. We should learn how to acquire assets instead of buying liabilities, which are things that decrease in value or decrease our net worth. We cannot be financially free with more debts than assets. Assets are the foundation of our financial freedom because they provide us with income for life.

3) The ability to raise private capital (or money)

We must cultivate good character and a good reputation so that we can raise capital from people we know. People like to deal with people they know and trust. Our character and reputation are the two pillars of our relationship with others when it comes to money. Sometimes, the only way to take advantage of a big opportunity is to share it with others. 50 percent of something is better than 100 percent of zero. The only way people will be involved in our financial transaction is if they trust your character and reputation, even though you might be skilled and know what you are doing. The better your reputation, the bigger your buying power can be. Other people's capital or money is an important factor in our business development and our buying power.

4) Institutional credit

The fourth part of our buying power can come from our ability to get credit with local banks and other public institutions or lenders. The economic or financial system of this world is based on credit and debt. In order to increase our credit lines and buying power, we must build relationships and great reputations with companies, banks, and lenders. These enterprises allow us to use their money for some fees and interest. They can help us greatly to achieve financial freedom quickly if we know how to manage money, our business, and ourselves. We need to pay great attention to our buying power. We need to manage our cash, assets, network, and our credit. These are the keys to our financial freedom. In the next chapter, we will look at credit and credit score.

Principles learned that you need to practice
* *Buying power, then, is the capability and power of purchasing things like cars, clothes, and foods.*

* *The value of all our assets increases our net worth if we keep our liabilities under control.*

* *People like to deal with people they know and trust. Our character and reputation are the two pillars of our relationship with others when it comes to money.*

* *The economic or financial system of this world is based on credit and debt. We need to build relationships and great reputation with banks, companies, and lenders to increase our credit lines and buying power.*

Your buying power is closely related to your credit. Let us go to the next chapter to look at the credit and credit score.

Chapter 12

Credit and credit score (The base of your financial life)

Financial term or concept 10: Credit and credit score

"Credit is the most important factor in every person's economic life." - Sezair Julien

The financial system of this world is based on credits and debts. If you take a deeper look at the capitalist system and the banking system, they are functioning on IOU certificates. The currencies used in all the countries around the world are nothing but pieces of paper with numbers printed on them. They are not backed by anything. This paper money, promised by the government, is called a note. You and I know that all governments are deep into debts around the world. Governments around the world have promised and credited the money system which keeps the financial system alive. The whole system is a big Ponzi scheme. So what is credit? Why is it so important to us? What is the credit score? Why is our credit score so important?

What is credit?
According to Finish Rich by David Bach, credit is the ability of a customer or someone to obtain goods and services before payment based on the trust that payment will be made in the future. The key words here are trust and before payment. The American Heritage dictionary also said that credit is the confidence in the trust of someone. The quality of being trustworthy. Again, the key word is trust. We must develop relationships and

trust with lenders, businesses, and people to increase and maintain good credit history.

In simple words, your credit gives you the opportunity to use other people's money to buy things or investment today and pay it back later or in the future. There are three types of credits: personal, business, and governmental. We are focusing on personal credit here.

Why is credit important to us?

Our credit is the most important part of our financial or economic life. The cost of using other people's money depends on our credit. Here are some of the things that our credit will and can do for us:

* Buy a car with a loan (lower interest and lower payment)
* Get student loan (afford an education)
* Rent an apartment (rent in better neighborhood)
* Get a business loan (lower interest rate, more choices)
* Investment loan (all kind of loans, credit line, lower interest rate, lower payment)

We need to keep track, manage, and control our credit on a regular basis. People, lenders, and creditors can check our credit by looking at our credit reports.

What is a credit score?

The credit score is a number assigned to a person that indicates to lenders his or her capacity to repay a loan according to Finish Rich Dictionary by David Bach. The credit score is a 3-digit number assigned to a person by FICO (Fair Isaac Corporation). According to David Bach, a credit score is based on factors such as a person's record for making timely payment, total debt, and credit history. It influences the person's ability to obtain a loan and the cost of the loan. The score is often called a FICO score because it is calculated using software from Fair Isaac Corporation.

The FICO score is a number between 300 and 850. The higher the number, the lower the risk that the borrower will default and the lower is the cost of borrowing money. The lower the number, the higher the risk to the lender that the borrower will default and the higher the cost of borrowing money. This shows how important our credit is to us. Credit can make one rich if we know how to use it properly.

How does FICO determine the credit score?

This score is determined by credit history. Here is how it is determined:

1) When someone buys something on credit, the company reports the balance to the credit bureaus: Experian, Equifax, and Transunion. The three credit bureau companies are private companies that collect all financial transactions about everyone in the economy in the US. They are like dumpsters who collect trash. These three companies collect and report all of our financial transactions on credit. They collect everything about the goods (good loans, credit cards, mortgages), the bads (late payments, collections), and the uglies (defaults, bankruptcies) about everyone.

2) The company we owe only sends our financial information to these three companies if we do not pay our bills on time, default, or file for bankruptcy. They, in turn, keep records on all these financial transactions to determine your credit score.

3) These three companies also sell your financial data to other institutions. This is their income strategy. It is all legal according to our government; the government gives these

companies the legal right to sell our financial information to other companies. The three credit bureau companies use the software from Fair Isaac Corporation (FICO) to calculate our credit scores. Based on our financial transaction they've received from us, each company assigns us scores. When a lender, for example, pulls our credit, the company receives three scores. Each number comes from each of the three credit bureau companies. The lender usually considers the middle score, not the lower or higher ones. The credit bureau also provides a report of all our financial transaction records to the lender.

Lenders and companies use the score to determine how much money that we are qualified for, the interest rates, and the cost associated with borrowing money. They also use our score to determine our credit worthiness. We need to keep track of our credit and we need to monitor closely what is on our credit report.

What is in the credit report?

The credit report is the record of all financial transactions done on an individual credit from mortgages to personal loans. This list is a comprehensive list of credit report components by order of importance:

* Payment history
* Percentage of credit used
* Hard inquiries
* Derogatory mark
* Total credit
* Total debt
* Account age
* Number of accounts
* Credit history

* Etc.

Our financial credit score is our passport number to a better finance and economic life. It is more significant than how much money you make. We need to know what our credit score is and, more importantly, what is in our credit history. Part of our financial freedom is to maintain a healthy credit.

What can we do to improve our credit?

Here is a list of things we can do to improve our credit score:

1) Order a credit report and start reviewing the report
2) Start cleaning the report
3) Pay down the higher balances
4) Pay the bills twice a month
5) Negotiate credit limit increase
6) Open new accounts
7) Negotiate outstanding balances
8) Become authorize users on other cards

Now, it is time to put into practice everything we learned in this chapter and the book.

Principles learned that you need to practice

* *Your credit gives you the opportunity to use other people's money to buy things or investments today and pay it back later or in the future.*

* *Your credit is the most important part of your financial or economic life. The cost of using other people' s money depends on our credit.*

* *The credit score is a number assigned to a person that indicates to lenders his or her capacity to repay a loan.*

* *The credit score is a 3-digit number assigned to a person by FICO (Fair Isaac Corporation). The FICO score is a number between 300 and 850.*

* *Lenders and companies use the score to determine how much money we are qualified for, the interest rates, and the cost associated with borrowing money.*

Chapter 13

Example Financial Statements: Income statement, Balance Sheet

The last chapter is all about examples. It is for you to practice and analyze these five examples of financial situations. This is one of the most important parts of the book. Practice does not make perfect, but practice does make improvement. Practice makes you challenge yourself. Studying, understanding, practicing, and teaching these 10 concepts will change your financial life forever. I guarantee it.

THE 10 CONCEPTS MODEL FOR YOUR FINANCIAL CHECK-UP

INCOME STATEMENT	BALANCE SHEET

INCOME	ASSETS	BUYING POWER
Active income	What you own	Liquid asset/ Credit
Passive Income	Income producing	Private/business credit
Business Income	Capital Gain	
(-)	(-)	

EXPENSES	LIABILITIES	CREDIT SCORE
Living Expenses	What you owe	Payment history
Taxes	Promises	Credit history
Luxuries	Good and bad Debt	
(=)	(=)	

CASH FLOW	NET WORTH
Surplus	Positive
Deficit	Negative

EXAMPLE 1:
Find out your starting point

INCOME STATEMENT	BALANCE SHEET

INCOME	ASSETS	BUYING POWER
Active: $ 6,000	$ 190,000	$ 45,000

(-)	(-)	
EXPENSES	**LIABILITIES**	CREDIT SCORE
Living: $ 4,800	$ 150,000	660
Luxury: $ 500		

(=)	(=)
CASH FLOW	**NET WORTH**
Surplus $ 700	+$ 40,.000

FINANCIAL CHECK-UP QUICK ANALYSIS

This person starts with a surplus of $700.00 a month, a net worth of $40,000.00, a buying power of $45,000.00, and a credit score of 660. His or her financial health is good. It can improve going forward.

We must focus our attention to this every month of our financial life. You must read this book as many times it takes to have these concepts become automatic in your life. This is the financial statement you need to give to lenders or lenders must put together for you to find out your financial health before lending you money. See more examples.

EXAMPLE 2
(take some time to analyze this financial statement)

INCOME STATEMENT	BALANCE SHEET

INCOME	ASSETS	BUYING POWER
Active: $ 10,500	Cash: $ 10,000	($ 300,000)
	401K: $ 150,000	

(-)	(-)	
EXPENSES	LIABILITIES	CREDIT SCORE
Tax: $ 2,000	Good: $ 508,.000	600
Living: $ 4,800	Bad: $ 34,000	
Luxury: $ 500		

(=)	(=)
CASH FLOW	NET WORTH
Deficit: ($ 700)	($ 384,000)

EXAMPLE 3
(take some time to analyze this second financial statement)

INCOME STATEMENT	BALANCE SHEET

INCOME	ASSETS	BUYING POWER
Active: $ 6,000	Cash: $ 10,000	$ 200,000
Passive: $ 6,200	Physical: $ 450,000	
Portfolio: $ 75	401K: $ 500	

(-)	(-)	
EXPENSES	LIABILITIES	CREDIT SCORE
Tax: $ 1,600	Good: $ 470,000	750
Living: $ 6,450	Debt: $ 500	
Luxury: $ 659		

(=)	(=)
CASH FLOW	NET WORTH
Profit: $ 3,535	$ 128,500

EXAMPLE 4
(Use this for your personal statement)

INCOME STATEMENT	BALANCE SHEET

INCOME	ASSETS	BUYING POWER

(-)	(-)	
EXPENSES	LIABILITIES	CREDIT SCORE

(=)	(=)
CASH FLOW	NET WORTH

EXAMPLE 5
(Use this to help your best friend with his or her financial statement and send him or her a copy of the book)

INCOME STATEMENT	BALANCE SHEET

INCOME	ASSETS	BUYING POWER

(-)	(-)	
EXPENSES	LIABILITIES	CREDIT SCORE

(=)	(=)
CASH FLOW	NET WORTH

Self-Publishing School

NOW IT'S YOUR TURN

Discover the EXACT 3-step blueprint you need to become a bestselling author in as little as 3 months.

Self-Publishing School helped me, and now I want them to help you with this FREE resource to begin outlining your book!

Even if you are busy, bad at writing, or do not know where to start, you CAN write a bestseller and build your best life.

With tools and experience across a variety of niches and professions, Self-Publishing School is the only resource you need to take your book to the finish line!

DON'T WAIT

Say "YES" to becoming a bestseller:

https://self-publishingschool.com/friend/

Follow the steps on the page to get a FREE resource to get started on your book and unlock a discount to get started with Self-Publishing School

ABOUT THE AUTHOR

Sezair Julien is passionate about helping others find their purpose in life and achieve financial freedom. To fulfill that passion, he has created the Financial Freedom Principles YouTube channel and Facebook group to teach and coach people on the principles required to practice being free in life. This book is the result of his experiences and his search for financial independence and freedom in life. This book is the beginning of many to come that will help you as well, to achieve your financial independence and your freedom in life.

After receiving my bachelor's degree in engineering and my master's in management, I was not satisfied with my finance and my freedom in life. I was enrolled in a PhD program when I quit to start a serious financial education that could lead to my freedom in life. I decided to become an entrepreneur, investor, a life student, a researcher of freedom principles, and a coach. My life has completely changed forever.

This book is helping me reach out to you and an invite to you to join me in this journey for freedom. The principles I practice in this book will change your life forever as well.

Can You Help?

Thank You For Reading My Book!

I really appreciate all your feedback, and I love hearing what you have to say.

I need your input to make the next version of this book and my future books better.

Please leave me an honest review on Amazon, letting me know what you thought of the book!

Thanks so much!

(Sezair Julien)